Your Portion of the Inheritance

Yinka Akintunde

YOUR PORTION OF THE INHERITANCE

YINKA AKINTUNDE

**RESOURCE HOUSE LTD
LONDON**

Copyright@ Yinka Akintunde 2011

All Rights Reserved

ISBN : 978-0-9568267-0-1

No part of this book may be reproduced in any form by photocopying or by any electronic or mechanical means, including information storage or retrieval systems without permission in writing from both the copyright owner and the publisher of this book.

First Published 2011 by
RESOURCE HOUSE LTD
P O BOX 944
Dagenham
RM9 9JW
United Kingdom

All Bible quotations have been taken from the New King James Version of the Bible, unless otherwise indicated in the text. 'KJV' refers to King James Version. 'Amp' refers to Amplified bible. 'NIV' refers to New International Version. 'NLT' refers to New Living Translation.

Printed for Resource House

Table of Content

Chapter 1 : It's About Inheritance..............01

Chapter 2 : The God Of Inheritance.......17

Chapter 3 : Through Christ Jesus...............27

Chapter 4 : There are More In There........41

Chapter 5 : And Even Much More............59

Chapter 6 : Partaker Not Spectator............77

Chapter 7 : The Word of Inheritance........93

Chapter 8 : It's Your Faith For Your
                                          Inheritance...............103

Chapter 9 : Patient Unto Inheritance.......117

Chapter 10 : The War Of Inheritance.......133

Chapter 11 : Divine Enabling For
                                          Inheritance...............149

Introduction

The Christian call is a call to an inheritance, made available by God through Christ Jesus. God as a father, in his kindness, demonstrated this at the beginning when he made all things needed for good living available in Eden before he called Adam into the scene. The sum total of what a Christian becomes is a function of how much of the inheritance of saints in Christ you are able to lay hold of and partake in on this side of eternity.

When people are born into natural families, especially the wealthy and noble ones, they are bestowed with a certain inheritance simply because they belong in that family. The inheritance might be material such as riches or it could be immaterial, such as status and privilege. When an individual in such family lays hold of his or her own inheritance and channels it right in life's pursuit, nobility and wealth are reproduced, propagated and perpetuated. Irrespective of your natural birth, once you are in Christ Jesus, you are an heir of God's family. You are a member of the ultimate nobility in heaven and on earth. The picture was painted better when your father, even God, ventured into the dark oblivion to create a home called earth for mankind in the beginning. He made everything good and made everything available, including fine gold, at creation before bringing you on the scene through mankind called Adam. Genesis 2:7-15.

Beyond the material world, in Eden, was also the power to dominate, blessing to flourish, and wisdom to succeed in spite of the devil lurking in the corner. Adam was brought into all of this, to have and possess as eternal inheritance for mankind. Genesis 1:26-30. It was in this inheritance Adam should have done his business and prospered, raised his family with no stress, lived a healthy life, dominated his environment and be what he was created and ordained to be. Chasing Adam out of the garden in the east of Eden after the fall was just a miniature of the bigger picture. What was lost in Adam was more than a garden with fruits, rivers, and gold. The reality was that humanity exited the inheritance from God in Adam at the fall. The loss of the inheritance that formed the foundation of human creation in the first place was the reason why human life on earth was plunged into ceaseless struggle, gloom, and doom in spite of a spirited effort to break even. Once the certainty of inheritance was lost, the gamble for survival became the order of the day. Making it or not, surviving or not, breaking even or staying down became a matter of luck and perhaps happenstance as it is seen today in our fast and furious world. If care is not taken, one can as well give up hope and assume the status of "not being lucky" in a world that comes across as callous and very partial.

My assignment in this book is to help you see beyond luck, which is an uncertainty, into a definite inheritance, which is sure, steadfast, and eternal. What you lost in first Adam has been recovered in the last Adam and even more was added. It is your duty to partake of and make same your present reality.

Chapter 1

It's About Inheritance

At midday, O king, along the road I saw a light from heaven, brighter than the sun, shining around me and those who journeyed with me. And when we all had fallen to the ground, I heard a voice speaking to me and saying in the Hebrew language, "Saul, Saul, why are you persecuting me?" It is hard for you to kick against the goads. So I said, "Who are You, Lord?" And He said, "I am Jesus, whom you are persecuting. But rise and stand on your feet; for I have appeared to you for this purpose, to make you a minister and a witness both of the things which you have seen and of the things which I will yet reveal to you. I will deliver you from the Jewish people, as well as from the Gentiles, to whom I now send you, to open their eyes, in order to turn them from darkness to light, and from the power of Satan to God, <u>that they may receive forgiveness of sins and an inheritance</u> among those who are sanctified by faith in Me"... Acts 26:13-18.

This is one of the most powerful accounts of a human encounter with God. The apostle made us see the content of the conversation that ensued and thus the subject matter. Jesus said the message of the gospel ought to turn people from darkness to light and from Satan to God. But he also would that all of this was done in order for the saved to receive an inheritance! Christianity can then said to be about obtaining the divinely bestowed inheritance. It is not about doctrinal argument. Apostolic grace as mighty as it was on Paul was said by the giver of grace himself to be used to help saints obtain their inheritance. To be turned from darkness to light and from Satan to God simply means to be saved. Jesus said men are saved to obtain or receive the inheritance laid up for those who are sanctified through faith in him. Simply put, you are saved to receive your own portion of inheritance among the saved. One will wonder why Jesus didn't say that men are saved to escape hell. He didn't say so because man was never made for destruction and condemnation. Hell or eternal doom was made for Satan and his angels. No wonder Jesus said that the only condemnation available is for someone to reject the grace of inheritance brought by him. **John 3:17-19.**

Called To Receive

Christianity is more than a religion. It is a call, a call by God through Christ Jesus unto all mankind from sin and darkness into light and his own righteousness. After Adam's fall in Eden, the only way out was to be called out by God. God did not come down immediately. Adam fell and was naked. God allowed Adam to do what a man in mess will do naturally. God allowed Adam to try and sort it out. So Adam sewed fig leaves for a covering. Many fig leaves of religion, philosophies, psychic empowerment, and all sorts of new age moves fill the world today to undo the evil deeds of the fall. As for Adam, the fig might cover the flesh but can't redeem the soul or revive the spirit. It may shield the flesh from shame but can't restore the lost glory. God then called Adam out of the struggle to fix him by himself.

Then the eyes of both of them were opened, and they knew that they were naked; and they sewed fig leaves together and made themselves coverings. And they heard the sound of the LORD God walking in the garden in the cool of the day, and Adam and his wife hid themselves from the presence of the LORD God among the trees of the garden. Then the LORD God called to Adam.... Genesis 3:7-9a.

The journey to recovery started for Adam the moment God's call was heeded (Adam means mankind). You might say, "*but god cursed them and judged them after calling them out.*" Yes you are right, but after all is said and done, before he let go of them, he helped them fix the mess they were trying to fix. He took the fig off and made coats of skin for them. It is true God is holy and hates sin. It is true he is the God of judgment, but be clear that God is all that and much more and is always there to help you fix your mess at the end of the day. Adam was hiding but the call found him out anyway. Many are hiding in a free-thinking godless world today, but the call of God through Christ Jesus is meant to find everyone out. In *the first Adam* humanity was called unto judgment, but in the *last Adam* which is Christ Jesus, humanity is called unto salvation through redemption. When someone heeds the call and is saved, he is then said to be one of the called.

For since, in the wisdom of God, the world through wisdom did not know God, it pleased God through the foolishness of the message preached to save those who believe. For Jews request a sign, and Greeks seek after wisdom; but we preach Christ crucified, to the Jews a stumbling block and to the Greeks foolishness, but to those who are called, both Jews and Greeks, Christ the power of God and the wisdom of God. Because the foolishness of God is wiser than men, and the weakness of God is stronger than men. For you see your calling, brethren, that not many wise according to the flesh, not many mighty, not many noble, are called...1 Corinthians 1:21-26.

Natural background or career achievement has nothing to do with the Christian call. Everyone is called but only few are chosen by heeding the call - a call from darkness into God's light, a call from Satan unto God, which is what the Christian call is.

It's About Inheritance

But you are a chosen generation, a royal priesthood, a holy nation, His own special people, that you may proclaim the praises of Him who called you out of darkness into His marvelous light...1 Peter 2:9.

Christians are not just called. They are called for a purpose. You are called out of darkness into light. You are not called out of darkness into oblivion. You are called into the spotlight. You are not called into light to just appreciate the light. You are called into the light to receive your own inheritance among them who are sanctified in light. **Acts 26:18**. To show forth the praises of him who called you out of darkness is to lay hold of the inheritance he bestowed in light and walk in them. This goes beyond singing praises. This is showing praise in a tangible sense. God's will is for you to show his praises once you are out of darkness, and Jesus said the way to do this is to receive what he had obtained for you in forgiveness as inheritance.

God called Abraham to bless him. When God called the children of Israel, he called them from what was bad into what was good, from bondage to liberty, from lack into abundance. Even though they saw the Red Sea parted, their call was not yet fulfilled since they had not come into their inheritance. All who died without entering Canaan were said to have perished in the wilderness. Christianity is a struggle in futility and an assault on the cost of redemption until you understand this concept. God's ultimate gift is not the freedom of his people from bondage as it were, but their eventual entrance into their glorious inheritance. Moses, while praying for God's mercy, said "No matter how much power you showed in parting the Red Sea, if you leave your people in the wilderness, the heathen around will say you are not successful in your rescue mission." Even though God judged those people, he made sure Caleb, Joshua and the people's offspring entered the Promised Land.

God saves to the utmost, he calls to give.

Called In Light

It is very important for you to know that the Christian call is a call into light and so everything made available therein is made available in light. The light in the context of inheritance is a position of illumination, a status based on knowledge and enhanced by the understanding of the plan purpose and provision of God for you in Christ Jesus.

Always thanking the Father. He has enabled you to share in the inheritance that belongs to his people, who live in the light....... Colossians 1:12 (NLT).

To live in light is to live in the place of knowing, a place of conscious awareness of where you belong and what belong to you in God. It is not good enough to know what God can do, it is necessary to know what you can do in God. It is not enough to know what God will do, it is necessary to know what you will do to be at the receiving end of what God will do. Most importantly, it is not good enough to know what God wants to do or what you want him to do, which is what many of us are concerned about. It is illumination to know what God has done already in Christ Jesus lest you are waiting for what has happened already to happen. The knowledge that brings to you the consciousness and awareness of who you are, where you are, and what you have in Christ by the reason of new birth is what can be accurately described as light. To live in light is to keep living out such knowledge and make it the compass of your journey in life no matter the wind you are sailing against. In as much as the inheritance is made available for God's people, the sharing of or partaking in it is a function of how much of your current life you live in light. It is important to note that Paul did not cease prayer for the saints in Ephesus once he heard of the zealousness so that their living in light could be enhanced by God's spirit and they can lay hold of the riches available for them in the inheritance.

For I always pray to] the God of our Lord Jesus Christ, the Father of glory, that He may grant you a spirit of wisdom and revelation [of insight into mysteries and secrets] in the [deep and intimate] knowledge of Him, By having the eyes of your heart flooded with light, so that you can know and understand the hope to which He has called you, and how rich is His glorious inheritance in the saints (His set-apart ones)...Ephesians 1:17-18 (AMP)

Once your eyes are flooded by the light, you are blinded to every other thing around you. The circumstances and inadequacies around you have little or no meaning to you again because you are transfixed in the flood of light. Your options are limited, and your steps are guided. The reason many lose out on the inheritance is because they can still see everything around them. They have many options and many alternate paths to follow. If God can't do it, their uncle can, so they can afford to turn right or left from the path of inheritance. When the eyes of your heart are flooded with divine light, like a deer on the road transfixed by a powerful headlamp in the night, you can't see any other thing; your gaze is fixed on what is fast coming your way. Your heart is flooded with the light of God coming your way; you are not shifting ground till the blessing of inheritance imparts you beyond recovery!

The light of God helps you to appreciate who you are in God and what is available for you in God. The same light helps you to see what it takes to lay hold of what has been provided. If there is struggle or dissatisfaction in one area of your life, same light helps you unravel the mystery and untie the knots. There is no complication of darkness that the light of God cannot sort out when allowed in.

Your word is a lamp to my feet and a light to my path...Psalms 119:105

God's word is the light in question. When the Holy Spirit grants you access to be imparted with the revelation knowledge of God's word, you will come into the understanding of what and the wisdom to appropriate your own lot or portion in the inheritance. The inheritance, therefore, does not exist in the realm of luck or wish. It is engraved in the word of God. No one enters the inheritance by sitting down and daydreaming. It is by making a lamp of life to walk by from the word of God. You are born again of the incorruptible seed of the word of God, said to be more precious than gold and silver. The same word is all you need to become what you are born to be. The Bible is not a history book or a theological book written for arguments and contention. It is light of life packaged in letter. The real labor in Christianity is to labor in the word, not for preaching but for living. Therein lies the meat that does not perish.

Eternal Reservation

**Blessed be the God and Father of our Lord Jesus Christ, who according to His abundant mercy has begotten us again to a living hope through the resurrection of Jesus Christ from the dead, to an inheritance incorruptible and undefiled and that does not fade away, reserved in heaven for you......
1 Peter 1:3-4**

When you were saved, you received eternal life, which is a kind of life that is not limited to this material world but penetrates into the heavenly where you are sitting with Christ in God. Your dimension of operation in life is therefore more than meets the eyes. Your level of riches, for example, is beyond the printed notes in your bank account or the material riches you currently possess. Have you read about the widow of a prophet whose material possessions on earth seem insufficient for her enormous debt and needs? As far as she was concerned, all she had for riches was a bottle of oil, but Elisha the prophet could see riches in the eternal realm reserved for her. Where do you think the oil was flowing from with which she paid her debt and lived by? God is too holy to steal someone else's oil for her! Riches were reserved for her that she could not see and so could not access. It took a man of the spirit to see it and channel it to her in tangible and material form flowing as oil. *2 Kings 4:1-7.*

The vitality in your body is beyond what the doctor's stethoscope and laboratory readings alone can determine. The life in King Hezekiah's body was almost exhausted due to a sickness he suffered, and so God told him to be ready to depart in the soon. After gaining access into the realm of eternity in prayer, more life was released from his account in the realm to last him another 15 years. *2 Kings 20:1-11.*

Your security is beyond the burglar proof and police protection. This sounds patronizing, you may say, but it is the reality of your heritage in God who in his wisdom choose not to leave all that accrues and pertains to you here on earth lest they become corrupted and compromised. Reserved for you in heavenly places is limitless inheritance, which you are expected to lay demand on or partake of while your sojourn here on earth lasts. Elisha, an Old Testament saint, saw into this realm once upon a time when it looked like he was outnumbered by the opposing forces. He, in confidence, told his servant to relax in the face of what looked like death and defeat because artillery reserved in eternity for the safety of saints on earth had just been dispatched for his safekeeping.

And Elisha prayed, and said, LORD, I pray, open his eyes that he may see. Then the LORD opened the eyes of the young man, and he saw. And behold, the mountain was full of horses and chariots of fire all around Elisha...2 Kings 6:17.

The language of the angel Gabriel to Mary concerning Elizabeth about the conception of John the Baptist will show you more clearly that laid up eternally for you are stuffs beyond people's verdict on you right now.

Now indeed, Elizabeth your relative has also conceived a son in her old age; and this is now the sixth month for her who was called barren.. Luke 1:36

She was called barren on earth by friends and foes including family doctors, but in eternity she was not called barren. John the Baptist was not an afterthought but a prophet ordained of God before he was formed in his mother womb. No wonder there is sarcasm in the language of the angel. She was without a child in time but was a mother of prophet in eternity. No wonder God admonished the barren here to sing as long as they can see beyond the medical reports. *Isaiah 54:1.*

You cannot just program your life around what is temporal or subject to change. There are things that are not seen that are eternal. These are contained in the inheritance said to be reserved for you, waiting to be laid hold of. That you don't see or feel them doesn't mean they do not exist. The things of the spirit are tangible, though they might need a material channel of expression to be seen, touched, or experienced here on earth. For example, the blessing of the lord is a tangible force of empowerment contained in the saints' inheritance, which when channeled into material endeavour produces riches and removes hurts.

The blessing of the LORD makes one rich, and He adds no sorrow with it...Prov 10:22.

What makes you thick is reserved or kept in eternity. Your life is not summed here on earth. Paul the apostle said if all that pertain to you is limited to this world, it is a miserable life. You have a heritage account in heaven you can draw upon here on earth when necessary for everything that pertains to life and godliness. You cannot afford to sum up your life based on what is visible and available here on earth. The real source and power behind your eventuality here on earth is stored up eternally.

In the Old Testament, all that was made known to mankind were the promises of God. The perfect will of God remained as great and precious promises until Christ came and fulfilled all righteousness thereby converting all God's great promises to inheritance for us. Anytime God made a promise in the Old Testament, he did so because what he was promising was already on ground. The promises were just to make man aware of the availability. He told Abraham, "*A father of many nations have I made you*" even when all Abraham could show for it were just promises upon promises. God promised he would pour his spirit in the last day upon all flesh, but the spirit has ever been available with God. He would not need to go and create the spirit in the last day. Everything that pertains to life and godliness had always been available with God in eternity, so he kept revealing them to humanity through great and precious promises until Christ Jesus came to make them our present reality. They are no more mere promises. They are our inheritance that we qualify for by simply being part of God's family or household. This is the reason why it is said that in Christ Jesus was fulfilled all the laws and prophecies.

As a Christian, you are not playing a game of claiming promises on God. You are out to obtain your own inheritance among those who are called and chosen. Everything you need is in your inheritance in the kingdom of God. This was why Christ forbade you from seeking material wealth as a priority but rather to seek your place in the kingdom where your eternal inheritance confers mastery over the temporal and material world. This material world comes from the eternal world of the spirit. God spoke the whole material world into existence from eternity. The good news is that the real you is with Christ right now in that realm, the same eternal realm where your inheritance is stored or reserved. The superseding ability of the eternal world on this temporary place was demonstrated after the initial creation when darkness took over the surface of the void and formless deep. God changed everything by his word and spirit. God allowed this account to be so in order for you to learn the curve of effecting changes on your temporal world using your eternal resources and abilities.

For 40 years, God fed about 3 million people with bread from heaven and didn't run out. This was to demonstrate the limitless, inexhaustible nature of eternal resources. Just because things are finished and dried here does not mean that they are dried and finished in the source. Jesus demonstrated this on various occasions. Once wine was finished, then appeared more wine again. There was a time when there was not enough bread and fish. Suddenly baskets of bread and fish were tumbling down from eternity. When Christ's disciples were outnumbered and seemingly out-equipped by the multitude that came to arrest Jesus, Peter tried to play the hero with his sword but Christ said there was no need. He told them that he could have asked for legions of angels to be sent from eternity for his rescue.

When you understand this concept of eternal inheritance, you will know that you cannot be in a fix without a way out. You can never be in need without a way out. You can never be outnumbered or successfully put down. The truth of the matter is that you can never be short of the capital and resources to fulfill your purpose on earth if you understand this concept well. Money is fleeting, but your inheritance of riches is forever. It stays in the family.

Promises can be claimed and used up, but the inheritance is eternal. Once you understand this, it stays in the lineage. You won't just experience prosperity but posterity to perpetuate eternal inheritance you have appropriated as a token of the goodness of the Lord. This is the difference between those who just chase money and those whose forefathers entered into the blessing of the Lord as an eternal inheritance. Years after they have gone, the inheritance still speaks in their lineage. This is what the scripture means when it says that *"the generation of the righteous is blessed."* In the Old Testament, when people walked with God and obtained an inheritance, maybe an office, a throne or blessing, it stayed in their family forever. Even when one generation was crooked and miss out in it, another set in the lineage that turned to God and walk with him would get it. This was why the scepter never departed from Judah or a law giver from his loin as he obtained it as a blessing of his father, Jacob. In reality, that blessing was not Jacob's blessing. He was just a conduit of the blessing. That blessing was God's blessing he bestowed on Abraham, which he passed down to Isaac and then to Jacob, and then Judah through David till it reached Christ Jesus, the Lion of the tribe of Judah. Maybe I should let you in on a secret. This same eternal inheritance is the reason why many offspring and generations of people who walked with God automatically entered into certain blessings with ease even more so than their progenitors who initiated the move, years after the initiators are gone. Reach out to the unseen but tangible inheritance laid up for you in heaven where you are called. It is eternal and can last for eternity in your lineage.

Chapter 2

The God Of Inheritance

So now, brethren, I commend you to God and to the word of His grace, which is able to build you up and give you an inheritance among all those who are sanctified...Act 20:32.

The sum total of all you can attain and obtain in life and eternity is summed up in the divine provision called your inheritance. This same inheritance is inherent in God. In the idolatrous but enlightened and philosophical Greek world, they had a faint glimpse of this as an unknown God in whom we ought to live and move and have our being. Paul, preaching the gospel in one of their cities, affirmed that they were not far from the truth - the fact that the God of inheritance they were talking about can be known and walked with.

God the Creator

God is not a name agreed upon at the United Nations to call a mysterious being hiding somewhere behind the clouds. God is the self-existing one who has no beginning or ending, nor source. He is the source of everything visible and invisible on earth and beyond, temporal and eternal. God was not advised to create man or anything. He was the one who thought it necessary and said let us create man in our image that they may possess everything on earth. He gave everything to man, including the free will to choose between good and evil. He appoints times and seasons. He is the monarch of the universe, nevertheless the earth and all that manifests therein he has given as an inheritance to man.

The heaven, even the heavens, is the LORD's; but the earth He has given to the children of men. Psalm115:16.

This is the reason why anytime God has to intervene supernaturally on earth, it is called a miracle because man has been given ownership here and helped to develop the wisdom needed to run it. The productivity and prosperity of this earth is entirely left unto man by God. This is why God is not jumping down to shake things when man gets it wrong. He would rather man develop the capacity to do it right. There is a part in God everybody owns, which is that part of God as the creator of all mankind. The religious and irreligious, he who offers oblation or he who offers blasphemy, God is the creator of all mankind. He rains on the good, the bad, and the ugly. He doesn't rain down hot sulphur on armed robbers and pedophiles while water falls on the farm of the good. He doesn't run his kingdom like men. Neither will he argue with a self-proclaimed atheist that he is a fool for being so myopic. He is the creator of all who has given the earth as an inheritance for all humanity to thrive upon no matter the race or creed. Nevertheless, there is another side to God wherein God comes across as a personal God and even more than a God, but as a father.

God The Father

We are God's begotten children through Christ. Adam was called God's son, same as Israel but we are different. We are begotten of the father, which means our substance literally came from his seed, which is the incorruptible word of God. We owe our fatherhood to God, and as his own children he has earmarked certain thing for us as inheritance to live by supernaturally. When a man's relationship with God revolves only around the physical things on earth, such a person is just a creation of God like everyone else. When a person's relationship with God as the father of all spirit goes beyond the veil of the flesh and earth but pierces into the realm of eternity and unseen where real inheritance are kept, such a one is a son of God.

The moment you came into God through Christ, you signed in for his will and purpose. Your aim is to be what he wants you to be, attain what he wants you to attain, and have what he wants you to have. You are not roaming the earth looking for mere survival. You are purpose driven. As you are conscious of the will of

God and driven by his purpose for your life, at the back of your mind you must know that you have obtained an inheritance with which to fulfill your mission.

In Him we have redemption through His blood, the forgiveness of sins, according to the riches of His grace which He made to abound toward us in all wisdom and prudence, having made known to us the mystery of His will, according to His good pleasure which He purposed in Himself, that in the dispensation of the fullness of the times He might gather together in one all things in Christ, both which are in heaven and which are on earth. In Him also we have obtained an inheritance, being predestined according to the purpose of Him who works all things according to the counsel of His will...Ephesians 1:7-11.

God is a spirit, so is your eternal inheritance. It is your duty to make it real and work for you when needed. In Christ, God built a bridge for you between all things on earth and in heaven where your inheritance is kept. Don't look down when the chips are down, rather look up. There is no point inheriting things from your parent if you won't make use of it. Many saints are going about life like orphans whose father didn't make any provisions whatsoever before discharging them to wander the planet earth. Many, therefore, depend on "luck" and all kind of uncertainty in living their lives. You are too blessed for that. God as a father made adequate provisions of inheritance for you in his *"will."* As you live out your purpose in this will, you ought to be unraveling and living on your inheritance.

It's God's Choice

Freedom and the ability to choose in life is a great feeling and worthy of appreciation. But in as much as we love to choose what we want, the reality is that we are not allowed to always do it. For example, you don't choose what family to be born into; you cannot choose your geographical place of birth or your race. The bitter truth is that you don't choose your sex either. You may manipulate your anatomy, but your genes and chromosomes are the same and intact to identify you as a male or female no matter the hormone therapy and surgery.

When it comes to what accrues to you in God as inheritance, you are not the one who chooses. God chooses for you according to his perfect will and purpose. Your part is to search it out and appropriate it. You, therefore, don't make life choice according to your neighbor's car and houses or choices. You are not allowed to envy or even compete with anyone because yours is loaded, too, only if you will sit down and appropriate what you have. The inheritance accrued to you is according to the race of life that is set before you. This is why God never set the race of life between but before us. Every man is on his own personal race. **Hebrew 12:1.**

You are running against you and no one else in life's race of destiny. This is why as a Christian; you ought not to join the rat race. You are the standard God will judge you by and not someone else. The reason someone will sit down and start clapping for himself because of some progress made in life till he loses a sea for a river is because most of the time he is measuring himself against others. Once he obtains a little than his neighbors he is comfortable, forgetting that to whom much is given so much is required.

Oh, clap your hands, all you peoples. Shout to God with the voice of triumph. For the LORD Most High is awesome; He is a great King over all the earth. He will subdue the peoples under us, and the nations under our feet. He will choose our inheritance for us, the excellence of Jacob whom He loves...Psalms 47:1-4.

As you can see, when it comes to everybody, God is a great king or overseer over all the earth. But when it comes to us his children, he is more than just a king ruling over an empire. He chooses our inheritance for us. He writes the script of your life for you to play out. He makes the costumes available as well to enhance your performance! The good news here is that his choices are excellent as you can read in that text. God is not a mediocre king, nor does he choose mediocre things as inheritance for his princes. One of the reasons why people detest divine choice is because they have assumed in their "unrenewed" mind that if it is godly, it must be terrible. So they would rather choose for themselves, live by themselves, and for themselves. The best of human choice will still rank far below God's any day. Who among us would want to make a foot stool and make one with a radius of about 6,371 kilometers, but that was what God did with the earth. **Isaiah 66:1.** None of us can build a city and make the street gold either, but that is what he did with the heaven. God has taste. It can be seen in the creation of humans, and you therefore can trust his choice. You are not on earth looking for dead meat like a scavenger. You are here to fulfill your glorious destiny making use of your God given inheritance.

...that we who first trusted in Christ should be to the praise of His glory...Ephesians 1:12.

This is the concluding part of the scripture we saw earlier talking about the will of God, the purpose of God, and the inheritance left for you in the will to fulfill the purpose. When you obtain and appropriate this, it gives God the glory.

Chose God First

If God is the source and architect of your inheritance in life and eternity, it is wise to win God first. It is better to gain God first. It is the best way to gain things and not lose your soul or the things gained at last.

After these things the word of the LORD came to Abram in a vision, saying, do not be afraid, Abram. I am your shield, your exceedingly great reward... Genesis 15:1.

You need to read the whole passage to know the dilemma of a man in need of material manifestation of what has been given to him in the spirit here. God called Abraham the father of many nations in eternity, but Abraham was still barren and he was feeling the pain and the void with the shame. No wonder the lamentation. God didn't rebuke Abraham for desiring what would give him joy and happiness as many of us think a "holy" God would have. God said, son, I understand your pain and shame, but gain me first. See me as not just a rewarder but as your reward. God said I will stoop so low as to be the trophy you will hold up as your gain for the race first before I give you Isaac, which you so desire, as part of the fringe benefits of gaining me.

No matter how big and precious your desires are; God said he is neither intimidated by them nor averse to them nor is he out to deny you. But you need to gain God first. What it means to gain God, you will ask. This is the same question Jesus answered when he was here on earth acknowledging the legitimacy of human material needs, and the way to go about it God's way.

Therefore do not worry, saying, what shall we eat or what shall we drink or what shall we wear, for after all these things the Gentiles seek. For your heavenly Father knows that you need all these things. But seek first the kingdom of God and His righteousness, and all these things shall be added to you...Mathew 6:31-32.

Jesus said, living for things to gain things is the unbelievers' way, but living for God to gain God and "all the things" he has in stock for you is your sure way out of the vicious circle. The word "seek" is not a nominal word. It is an active word that requires effort, time, and resources. You are to seek God to find and gain him. You are to also seek his way to do it right in life. Having been born of God, the responsibility is now on you to discover God in you through his word and develop a relationship with him by the Holy Ghost. There is God's right way of getting money, there is his right way of running a home, pursuing a career, being a boss, being a servant, being an husband, being a wife, running a business, being healthy, winning battles, and so on. God's righteousness or right standing and right way of doing things covers all spheres of life you live here. Nothing is left undone by Christ or untouched by God. It is your duty to discover God in that area and gain him to your side. If you gain God to your side in any area, the fringe benefits of such areas will automatically come. If there is endless struggle with no light, you have not discovered God there. Seek first the kingdom of God there and his right way of approach and all these things you are crying and panting for will be added. Instead of getting angry with everything and everyone, this is a better and sure way about life.

O Lord, you are the portion of my inheritance and my cup, you maintain my lot. The lines have fallen to me in pleasant places; yes, I have a good inheritance... Psalms 16:5-6.

This is the end of all hustling and struggles in life! Can you imagine God maintaining your lot for you? You cannot be cheated in life nor can you lose out in any way. If there is any set back, you can see it as a set up for speed and heights because God maintains your lot. Your lot in your body, in your children, job, business, career, socially, among foes and friends. On earth, in heaven, and beneath the earth, God stands as the one who maintains your lot so you won't be robbed or cheated. You can hustle and struggle to get things, but hustling and struggling won't keep them safe. You can hustle to gain material wealth, but to live in health, safety, and soundness of mind to enjoy it is another ball game beyond your control, an absolute gift from God. You can hustle to build a home or city but unless the Lord watches over it, crumbling is inevitable. I grew up in a part of the world where, for obvious reasons, the leaders loved building new projects rather than maintaining the existing ones. What eventually happens is the decadence and needless waste of both new and old. They had the capacity to build but lacked the initiative and good will to maintain. In your case, not only will God choose the right lots for you, he will stand as a defender and maintainer of the same lots against the onslaught of the wicked one. This is eternal security flowing out of eternal inheritance toward you!

Chapter 3

Through Christ Jesus

Adam, meaning mankind, was given the ownership of the earth and bestowed with all that would make things work here on earth. Part of what he received was a blessing, which is not a material thing. He had all the material things created for him even before he came on the scene, but the blessing was an empowerment to be fruitful, multiply, and replenish. Even though Adam was given everything, he could not maintain it or, better put, he lost it. Over a period of time, God released bit and pieces to people in various dispensation until Christ came on the scene as the last Adam.

Just as it is said, *"physician heal your own self,"* Christ was first given a name that is above all names. The name Jesus was obtained by Christ as an inheritance, even though an angel told Mary what name the holy seed would bear and the meaning. Giving the name Jesus to Christ by his parents was not enough for that name to be a name above all names.

God, who at various times and in various ways spoke in time past to the fathers by the prophets, has in these last days spoken to us by His Son, whom He has appointed heir of all things, through whom also He made the worlds: who being the brightness of His glory and the express image of His person, and upholding all things by the word of His power, when He had by Himself purged our sins, sat down at the right hand of the Majesty on high, having become so much better than the angels, as He has by inheritance obtained a more excellent name than they...Hebrews 1:1-4

Christ obtained his name as an inheritance. That we can pray in Jesus's name today and cast demons in his name is not a coincidence or religious fallacy, it is a fact of life. How did Christ obtain his name as an inheritance? Through obedience unto God by yielding himself to God's perfect will in dying for mankind's sin on the cross.

Let this mind be in you which was also in Christ Jesus, who, being in the form of God did not consider it robbery to be equal with God, but made Himself of no reputation, taking the form of a bondservant, and coming in the likeness of men. And being found in appearance as a man, He humbled Himself and became obedient to the point of death, even the death of the cross. Therefore God also has highly exalted Him and <u>given Him the name</u> which is above every name, that at the name of Jesus every knee should bow, of those in heaven, and of those on earth, and of *those under the earth, and that every tongue should confess that Jesus Christ is Lord, to the glory of God the Father...Philippians 2:5-11.*

I have heard of a few deluded celebrities who compared themselves to Christ because they were popular in their country, the western world in particular. Some of them have not even been to nor known till now in some backside of African or Asian villages and yet they feel they are more popular than Christ. Yet, Christ Jesus's name has spanned over many generations. All efforts to stop it by the various forces in the past and the present, including the modern-day godless voices, have never seen an iota of success. Christ's name is not just known. Jesus Christ's name saves and is a strong tower multitudes run into daily for safe keeping.

Not only did Christ obtain the name unto himself through death, he by the same death became the source of salvation and eternal inheritance to them who are saved. Talking about the same Christ, the scripture has this to say:

And for this reason He is the Mediator of the new covenant, by means of death, for the redemption of the transgressions under the first covenant, that those who are called may receive the promise of the eternal inheritance...Hebrews 9:15.

The inheritance was lost through transgression under the first covenant, He, by death, bought everything back (redemption). Not only did Christ save you and secure your inheritance for you, he also reconciled you and made you to be one at peace with the God of inheritance.

Which Inheritance

Then I looked, and I heard the voice of many angels around the throne, the living creatures, and the elders; and the number of them was ten thousand times ten thousand, and thousands of thousands, saying with a loud voice: Worthy is the Lamb who was slain to receive <u>power</u> and <u>riches</u> and <u>wisdom</u>, and <u>strength</u> and <u>honor</u> and <u>glory</u> and <u>blessing</u>!...Revelations 5:11-12.

Christ received them, but he does not need them. He lives as a spirit in eternity. What would he do with the blessing? He is the all-powerful God in the first place. What would he do with power or riches? He obtained all the above for you, hallelujah! Christ Jesus being God and man did not obtain these things as God for God, Just as he was not slain as God but as man called precious Lamb of God. It was the man Jesus who died, and he died because of mankind, not for himself or for angels. Everything Jesus obtained through his death he obtained for mankind. These seven powerful entities underlined above are what constitute the inheritance of the saints. Everything you need now and for eternity is summarized in those seven items, which make up the inheritance of the saints. All material and immaterial elements answer to those seven.

Your eternal rest in glory with God is in them. Let us see the content of your inheritance:

The Heritage of Power

The ability to effect change is what power is, in this context positive change, and that is what Christ gave you.

And Jesus came and spoke unto them, saying, all power is given unto me in heaven and in earth...Matthew 28:18 (KJV)

Having died, resurrected, and gone to the father to obtain the eternal inheritance for you, Jesus made this profound pronouncement that all power signifies that there is only one authentic power in which all other powers that be are sourced. Immediately after that statement he said, "go and be the representation of that power all over the place." It is therefore not flattering to say you have power as part of your heritage. What power, you will ask.

(i) Power of Life and Death

God literally handed over the power of life and death to Adam, but he thought lightly of it. God didn't kill Adam, nor did the devil. Adam self-destructed. He had the power of life and death in his hands. God said the day you eat the fruit you will initiate death or bring death into existence, and that was what Adam did, unfortunately. That was the power Satan stole with deceit from Adam and started tormenting humanity with from then on through fear. Ranging from spiritual death, which is separation from the life of God, to physical death, which had a sting - death was set in array against mankind until Christ came on the scene. He simply destroyed or conquered Satan who stole the power of death through deceit from Adam by his own death.

Inasmuch then as the children have partaken of flesh and blood, He Himself likewise shared in the same, that through death He might destroy him who had the power of death, that is, the devil, and release those who through fear of death were all their lifetime subject to bondage... Hebrews 2:14-15.

Now you are free from death, including its pain and the sting there. You are spiritually alive to God by new birth and free from physical death because you will only sleep when your time to depart the body comes. Jesus made a profound statement that Satan and humans who could kill the physical body only have one power with them, which is the power of the first death. He further said that God has the power of first and second death whereby he can destroy the soul in eternity after physical death on earth. Now that Christ has obtained all power, including the power of life and death in your favor, you are not just free from the sting of the first death. You will be eternally free from the second death if you hold on to Christ your savior. The other good thing is that death has no right to stop you from fulfilling your purpose here on earth. When you depart here, it must be because you have finished and accomplished your assignment here and duly qualify for rest. This shows that you cannot die before your time. No sickness is terminal in your case. No matter how bad the case might be now, you shall live and not die until you finish your assignment. This was the depth of revelation Paul had, and he was toying with death at will. He was stoned to death once and he was certified dead because the disciples were already planning his burial, but then he stood up. *Acts 14:19-20*. What about the injuries, you ask. Everything disappeared because death was not allowed to have the final say. Injuries and bodily damage by sickness are only needed by death to declare the body as incapable to house human spirit on earth any longer. Refuse to give in to death, no matter the condition of your body right now. Insist on life, healing, repair, and restoration of your body. The sickness will go and your body will be healed, and death will stop hanging around in the mighty name of Jesus Christ. Life and immortality was brought to an accessible point for you through empowerment by the death, burial, and resurrection of our Lord Jesus.

For God has not given us a spirit of fear, but of power and of love and of a sound mind, therefore do not be ashamed of the testimony of our Lord, nor of me His prisoner, but share with me in the sufferings for the gospel according to the power of God, who has saved us and called us with a holy

calling, not according to our works, but according to His own purpose and grace which was given to us in Christ Jesus before time began, but has now been revealed by the appearing of our Savior Jesus Christ, who has abolished death and brought life and immortality to light through the gospel 2 Timothy 1: 7-10.

(ii) Power to Become

One of the inherent abilities in power is in its capacity to change the state of or transform things from what they are to what they ought or intend to be. God would have us transformed from whatever we were to what he wants us to be. For example, from a mere creation to a new creation, even his own sons.

But as many as received him, to them gave the power to become the sons of God, even to them that believe on his name: which were born, not of blood, nor of the will of the flesh, nor of the will of man, but of God...John 1:12-13.(KJV)

The word "sons" has nothing to do with gender as in male child. It means mature ones who could be given the ownership and control of the father's business and inheritance. Accepting Christ into your life automatically confers on you the status of being born of God. As you can see in the text, they "were born" of God already, but are "to become sons of God." You don't need to become what you were already, so the text makes us realize that new birth through faith in Christ confers on you the birth from God. The power Christ gives you is part of your inheritance that will work out the *"sonship"* in you. The power brings you to the place of growth and maturity whereby you can take ownership and control of the father's business on earth.

Not only will the power help you to mature, but it is given to help you become whatever you ought and want to become in life. *You are never powerless or helpless in your purpose.* Once you discover your purpose in God and pursue it according to his good will, you should not see yourself as limited and incapacitated again. I know your feelings and even some unpleasant experiences might say so, but the reality is you are being given the limitless power to become what you ought to become. While on earth, Jesus called some men to become preachers, a total departure from what they used to be. Having learned the nuances of ministry and witnessing from him over years, it was obvious Jesus was no longer going to be around with them. They looked at the situation around; saw the obvious disadvantages, the political situation in their land and the obvious oppressive tendencies of their leaders. They went about trying to figure out how they would be able to become what the master said they were called to be and concluded that political emancipation and leadership overhaul should be a starting point. They then asked the master when the oppressive Roman Empire would be kicked out by God and the economy would recover, among many other things. Jesus, in his usual manner, gave them an odd answer.

Therefore, when they had come together, they asked Him, saying, Lord, will you at this time restore the kingdom to Israel? And He said to them, it is not for you to know times or seasons which the Father has put in His own authority. But you shall receive power when the Holy Spirit has come upon you; and you shall be witnesses to Me in Jerusalem, and in all Judea and Samaria, and to the end of the earth...Acts 1:6-8.

As good and desirable a conducive political milieu is, Jesus said that would not be the determinant of you becoming what you are created and called to be. He said all you need is to be empowered against all odds. He said once the power is at work in you, you will be unstoppable by politics or geography. Your success will be across human or natural boundaries. You will be able to go as far as you wish, as far as you can imagine.

In your inheritance is the power to become what you are meant to be irrespective of the odds and circumstances that stand against your chance from the human perspective. The ability to forge ahead against all odds, the capacity to conceive and give birth to dreams and visions in your life's pursuit is what we refer to as power. Praise God it is part of your inheritance. If you are in business, the same power will move your business forward and make it what it ought to be. If you are in any career, the same power that helped those in ministry build a successful ministry is the same power given to you to make a success out of your career.

When we talk of power, people generally think about pastors, evangelists, preaching, people think of being slayed in the spirit and all those things genuine and spooky, within the four wall of the church. But far from it. The power is given to us all to be witnesses. But what witness, and what are we witnessing? The word "witness" does not just refer to someone who is talking about something. It is also someone who represents or stands as a testimony to validate the reality of something or an event. You are empowered by God to validate the fact that Christ died for your sin, weakness, inadequacies, sickness, failure, and shortcomings as human. Not only are you to validate or be a witness to the death of Christ, you are much more a witness to his conquest through burial resurrection and accession far above all principalities and powers that be. In essence, you are a witness to the complete, limitless, and abundant life Christ had brought to light in dealing with all human shortcomings. The power in your inheritance is to help you live and make these true in your daily experience while on earth, effecting positive change in and around you.

(iii) Power Over The Enemy

Behold! I have given you authority and power to trample upon serpents and scorpions, and [physical and mental strength and ability] over all the power that the enemy [possesses]; and nothing shall in any way harm you..... Luke 10:19 (Amp).

The whole human history cannot be complete until we mention the enemy. Everything changed in humanity once the enemy came on the scene. The whole story changed in Eden from the beginning of Genesis chapter 3 when the enemy was introduced as the serpent. Adam's household wasn't the same after he made an ally of the enemy. When Christ came on the scene to undo the damage initiated by the enemy, the first thing he received for you as inheritance was power. Inherent in this power is the dominion or authority over the enemy. Not only did Christ defeat the enemy, he also obtained power over the enemies and his coalition forces for you in case they rear their ugly head. Satan is the enemy. His coalition forces include demonic entities in their hierarchy. It can also include human agents and your own flesh. All of these are called the "powers of the enemy." As wicked as they are, you only need one power to subdue and dominate them all and this same power is what Christ got for you as an inheritance.

The authority is the permission to do, while the power is the ability or capacity to carry it out. Jesus got you the permission or right to subdue the hurting power of the enemy. He also got you the capacity and ability to do the same. You ought not to live in fear anymore. You cannot afford to keep thinking of what and who is against you and wanting to stop your progress. You ought to be dominion-minded, knowing fully that you are immune to all hurt by the reason of your inheritance of power. He didn't say the enemy or his agents will not want to hurt you, but he said you are too empowered to be hurt or harmed in any way by the powers of the enemy. Your inheritance puts you above all opposition and puts the enemy at your mercy. The same power is the power with which you subdue your flesh when the enemy wants to work through it to truncate your destiny. The devil energizes the flesh unto sin to put you in the same platform as the children of disobedience. When the scripture says sin shall not have power or dominion over you, it is with the understanding that you have power over Satan who is the root and the flesh which is the agent of sin he employs.

Yinka Akintunde

CHAPTER 4

THERE ARE MORE IN THERE

Then I looked, and I heard the voice of many angels around the throne, the living creatures, and the elders; and the number of them was ten thousand times ten thousand, and thousands of thousands, saying with a loud voice: Worthy is the Lamb who was slain to receive power and riches and wisdom, and strength and honor and glory and blessing!...Revelations 5:11-12.

The Heritage of Riches

Material and immaterial riches are part and parcel of your inheritance as a saint of the lord.

And my God shall supply all your need according to His riches in glory by Christ Jesus...Philippians 4:19.

The subject matter here is all of your needs. God's riches are made available to you as inheritance to meet all your needs as you live in this material world. The reality is that though you live in a material world, all your needs are not material. Jesus said God is not a hypocrite. He knows you live in a material world and so will need material supplies to meet your material necessities and needs. But beyond material needs are your security needs, physical needs (health and well-being), emotional needs, and social needs. God does not want you to have one and leave the others suffering or unattended to in your life. People have by the reason of care of what shall we eat and how shall we be clothed (material needs) ruined some other aspect of their lives. People seek money and get killed in the course of doing so. Others have lost their precious relationship to material pursuit and vice versa. God wants you to strike a balance in your life. The way out is to seek God and his right way of doing things (God's kingdom and its righteousness). You will learn God's way for you to prioritize, pursue, and dispatch material and immaterial riches as you do so.

Material Riches

Although you are a spirit being, you live in a material body that needs to be attended to by the material world. Your soul, which includes your mind, will, and emotion, responds to the material world based on signals sent to it by your body senses. This connection is the reason why you "feel hungry" even though what was lacking was not a feeling but a material presence of food in your stomach. The presence or absence of material supplies to meet your material needs has a way of affecting your emotions or feelings, which invariably will affect the condition of your mind to dispatch your will in making a decision to do or not do certain things. God is the one who created human wiring this way. If he hadn't, we would walk into fire, sleep in the cold, or starve our body unto destruction.

To meet your material needs, which God duly recognizes as legitimate and needful, the riches of inheritance are channeled to you in various ways. Food, shelter, money, and all material riches you need in this world are channeled to you through your inheritance, but they don't drop physically from heaven. If money dropped once we prayed, human minds would atrophy and this world would go into decay. When riches come as part of your inheritance from on high, they will still need a channel of conversion into material and tangible wealth for you to enjoy it. The only and authentic channel approved by God to get material riches on earth is the channel of productivity. This is the reason why many saints pray, fast, and even give and there is no material wealth to show for it. If God allows food to appear on people's tables by prayer and transportation under them by fasting, the world would not be replenished as ordained, and there would be no development or evolvement of human minds. We would still be riding horses from New York to

London, wasting our time and endangering our lives. The riches of God are then channeled through the human mind by way of productivity to find solutions to the needs on earth and thereby rewarded with the attending material riches. Think of it, the technician who finds solutions to your motoring need when your car develops a problem will be rewarded with your money whether you love him or not.

Therefore you shall keep the commandments of the LORD your God, to walk in His ways and to fear Him. For the LORD your God is bringing you into a good land, a land of brooks of water, of fountains and springs, that flow out of valleys and hills; a land of wheat and barley, of vines and fig trees and pomegranates, a land of olive oil and honey; a land in which you will eat bread without scarcity, in which you will lack nothing; a land whose stones are iron and out of whose hills you can dig copper. When you have eaten and are full, then you shall bless the LORD your God for the good land which He has given you........ Deuteronomy 8:6-10.

These people had been fed and clothed miraculously for 40 years, but God said that was not his perfect plan for them. He wanted them to plant crops, dig brass, and work by their own hands and reap the fruits of productivity. The manna could not make them rich. It was merely a welfare package for a crisis period. God had the power and unlimited supply to have kept them on manna and quail forever, but that is not God's way. No one wants an idle man for an heir! This same passage is where God said they now had the power to get wealth, but we can see that if they wanted brass or any mineral they had to dig for it. Any gem they refused to discover and dig would remain under the soil while they suffered lack and poverty even though they had been given power to get wealth. On earth it takes both mental and physical activities for money and material riches to find an expression in the hand of a saint, even though you have an inheritance of riches in Christ. Jesus could have waved his hand in the air and money would appear, but he told Peter to go and fish in order to find money for their taxes. This taught us the lesson that money will not appear under your pillow while praying and sleeping, go out and work, saint! They were busy idling, talking, and waiting for rapture in Thessalonica, and Paul said such lazy ones don't have to wait for rapture any longer, as they will die of hunger anyway as long as they refuse to work, ***2 Thessalonians 3:10-12.***

Food here includes clothing, shelter, cars, and other material riches. Anyone who refuses to be productive does not deserve the riches. What about the disabled and aged people, you will say. That is why the word of God distinguished between those who refuse to work and those who are unable to work. Some are incapacitated by age, sickness, disabilities, war and other circumstances beyond their control. These are not the ones who refuse to work. If you understand this revelation, this will terminate unemployment in your life once you are fit and able. The reason is that you can only refuse to work under the covenant once you are able. There is no room for unemployment in your case. You will always find something to do!

Avoid the Pitfalls

Because we live in a material world, the devil uses material riches essentially as a trap for the souls of all human, sinners, and saints alike, but light will make a difference in your case. The enemy has built deceit around money and material riches so much that he has to be exposed. There are two extremes on riches where deceit dwells. The first one is to think that you don't need riches or that God does not care about you having material riches or that God cares but is helpless to give you material riches. All of these are lies of the devil. This is why many Christians are rather comfortable with unbelievers having material riches rather their own brothers and sisters becoming materially rich. They will criticize rich saints and clap for wealthy sinners and even make a testimony if such attend a special church program. This same deceit is why people equate lack and poverty to godliness and a requisite to going to heaven. Thank God this has changed much in the body of Christ over time.

Here is what I have seen: it is good and fitting for one to eat and drink, and to enjoy the good of all his labor in which he toils under the sun all the days of his life which God gives him; for it is his heritage. As for every man to whom God has given riches and wealth, and given him power to eat of it, to receive his heritage and rejoice in his labor—this is the gift of God...Ecclesiastes 5:18-19.

The second extreme is where money and God are placed on the same platform and people would even rather have the money than please God. This is the place where people can do anything for money, bad or evil. It is sad to see young Christians chasing money at the expense of their souls, just like unbelievers. When I got saved, you could leave a sack of money with brothers and sisters and not bother to count on collecting it back and everything would remain intact. This naivety was my mindset when I left the university until I started falling victim of frauds from believers, which is very sad. Many young Christians have been taken in by the deceitfulness of riches that they are all over the Internet looking for who to dupe out of their money. This shouldn't be. Kenneth E. Hagin of blessed memory talked of sharp practices in giving and receiving money in churches in his days and how he almost didn't want to have anything to do with money and giving matters in order to avoid the smear. He said God then asked him not to leave it entirely to the fraudulent ones and rob saints of their blessings but to walk in the middle of the road and teach it right. I got the rudest shock of my life as a young zealous minister in 1993 when the pastor I was serving under offered the church up for sale. I saw how various bidders came in and how the flock of Christ was being haggled. I felt bad and have still hardly recovered. We were eventually sold to the highest bidder as a congregation, and I felt helpless being less knowledgeable in the things of God.

Many sharp practices are all over the altar today because of the deceitfulness of Satan about riches. Paying a tithe does not sanctify or make stolen wealth or drug money holy and acceptable to God. It is deceitful to steal for God. Money will not and cannot meet all human needs. The deceit of the devil is to make you think that once you have enough money, all your problems and challenges are solved. He therefore makes you seek it with anything at the expense of everything.

Someone can make money at the expense of true advancement in life's journey to destiny. In Christ, what matter to you is real gain that comes with godliness rooted in contentment. When your heart's desire and thirst is not the quantity of riches in your hand but in God who gives much and little and yet meets all needs anyway, you will find true contentment and make great gains or advancements in the journey of destiny.

Command those who are rich in this present age not to be haughty, nor to trust in uncertain riches but in the living God, who gives us richly all things to enjoy. Let them do good, that they be rich in good works, ready to give, willing to share, storing up for themselves a good foundation for the time to come, that they may lay hold on eternal life...1 Timothy 6:17-19.

Material riches without godly purpose are a trap to rob you of eternal life. Watch the pit falls.

Immaterial Riches

Part of your inheritance in Christ is immaterial riches. The angels are given as security to guard you against harm. They see to it that you are protected against seen and unseen forces of destruction. You must believe in and keep your ministering spirits or angel active by your word.

Righteousness peace and joy in the Holy Ghost are given as the kingdom treasures to cascade in your inner man in order for you to be free from depression and oppression of the wicked. As a saint, you must have a rich soul, buoyant in joy and emotion irrespective of the circumstances around you. No wonder the joy of the lord is said to be your strength.

Your health and well-being is paramount to God as a caring father. He makes available for you healings and health as part of the riches of your inheritance. All of the germs and free radicals roaming your body are not enough to exhaust the divine provision for your health. You can therefore lay demand on this in the face of sicknesses and diseases and expect to be made well.

You are not of the World but you are the light and salt of the World. The World needs you to add value and contribute positively to it. Christians are not pariahs to development and a nuisance to society. You are an addition to the goodness, a person of value. Inside of your inheritance is your social riches, which as you explore, and live out, the world, will start finding help in you as the salt of the heart. In your place of work, local community, and the society at large, your calling is to contribute to the value of human life and improve existence with your rich social contribution to the evolvement and goodness of mankind. For you, it is not enough to have riches. It is also necessary to do well to others. It is not enough to serve God as a spiritual being. It is necessary to serve God through humanity as help and light giver. Giving to the poor, helping the needy, volunteering in service of humanity while expecting nothing back is part of your call and inheritance. Radiating positive energy in the company of others rather than causing gloom and depression are part and parcel of the riches of your Christian inheritance. You are meant to be the hope not part of the complaint when the chips are down.

Remember that when the party was about to spoil, Jesus your master brought back the sweetness as wine by exerting his influence on what was available, which was water. You are not expected to save the world and lose your own family. You are given divine help to build healthy personal relationships in marriage (if married), parenting (if you are one), and be fulfilled all the way.

The Heritage of Wisdom

The world you are living in is a product of divine wisdom. God crafted the world by wisdom, and by wisdom he expects you to live successfully therein. This wisdom includes common sense but it is still far and higher than common sense. This wisdom is not cunning but pure and peaceable wisdom of God, which comes to you by his word and through his spirit. Looking at the story of creation, one can say, what a massive display of power by God. But in as much as there was power manifestation, the whole issue was not rooted in power but in wisdom. The darkness and the void gave way to wisdom and not power. The emptiness in the begining was filled with beautiful things called creation through wisdom. Pattern came into a world without form by wisdom.

The LORD by wisdom founded the earth; by understanding He established the heavens; by His knowledge the depths were broken up, and clouds drop down the dew... Proverbs 3:19-20

O LORD, how manifold is thy works! In wisdom hast thou made them all: the earth is full of thy riches...Psalms 104:24

This is the equation. The earth that was given to mankind in Adam as an inheritance was a product of wisdom. It would therefore take wisdom to thrive in it against all odds. No wonder God did not lay emphasis on power when he was handing over the garden to mankind. God's emphasis was on wisdom to dwell during the handling over ceremony. God gave everything to Adam and gave him instruction of wisdom on how to safely dwell in prosperity without death shame or toil. When Satan came on the scene, he didn't come for the power and might of Adam. He didn't come shaking trees and causing chaos. He came for the wisdom with which Adam kept the earth in blessing and corrupted it. The wisdom of God was simply hidden in the instruction. Don't eat the fruit and you will not activate death. It sounded too stupid for common sense, Satan said. Eat the fruit and the nutrients will make you as wise as God. After all, he created it in the first place.

Thank God for Christ. He abolished death and defeated Satan forever by wisdom as well, using death to destroy him who had the power of death and wisdom to destroy him who had subtlety.

But we speak the wisdom of God in a mystery, even the hidden wisdom, which God ordained before the world unto our glory, which none of the princes of this world knew: for had they known it, they would not have crucified the Lord of glory... 1 Corinthians 2:7-8.

Christ is the wisdom and power of God. He therefore needed no wisdom himself. Yet according to our anchor scripture, he got them as inheritance. The only reason for him to have received wisdom is to bequeath the same to you as your inheritance. Wisdom is the antidote to darkness, emptiness, and the void. When life seems empty and void of good results, what you need to lay hold of is the wisdom in your heritage. When darkness of depression and confusion build siege around your mind or life, have it at the back of your mind that you have the wisdom of God that fixed darkness in the beginning as your heritage. You are not running from pillar to post for the wisdom. You are simply discovering the riches of your inheritance in Christ as you line up for divine wisdom. Wisdom will put three major things in your hand:

<u>Wisdom Will Give You Wealth</u>

Mental resources and ideas that create material wealth are hidden in wisdom. The quantum of forces applied in the market place of life is not what determines the output delivered but rather how the forces are applied. Two people can put in the same hours and same effort in the same business under the same circumstances and still get different results based on how they went about applying the effort. Wisdom will put in your hand the knowhow to maximize profit on any given task. When all natural resources of wisdom and knowledge have been exhausted, the supernatural wisdom of God will put in your hand the key to unravel knotty issues of life. While others hang their heads in frustration, you shall be shouting, lifting is yours. Walking in this wisdom, you will not move into business or a venture because it is in vogue or attractive. You will invest your efforts and resources somewhere because you are guided from within to do so. I remember growing up in a society where virtually everyone, including the educated, wanted their children to be a doctor, a lawyer, a pharmacist, or an engineer, in that order. Many destinies were derailed while some are even still tied down to what was in vogue with no material or non-material fulfillment to show for it until now simply because they were hapless wards forced to pursue the wrong path. You might stumble on profits in another area while doing what you know is the right thing, but life must not be a gamble for you as a believer. What rescues you from gambling your way through is called wisdom. You know what to do and how to do it. You can do it right the first time. I have heard people blame capital for failure in business, but the prodigal son had capital and probably even too much of it. What he lacked was wisdom because the Bible said he wasted his substance, which is an express reflection of lack of wisdom.

Happy is the man who finds wisdom, and the man who gains understanding; for her proceeds are better than the profits of silver and her gain than fine gold. She is more precious than rubies, and all the things you may desire cannot compare with her. Length of days is in her right hand, in her left hand riches and honor. Her ways are ways of pleasantness, and all her paths are peace. She is a tree of life to those who take hold of her, and happy are all who retain her...Proverbs 3:13-18.

If, for instance, you want to start an entrepreneurial endeavor and you don't have enough money in your account or no money at all, but you have bars of gold, balls of silver, and some other precious gem in your safe somewhere. If out of frustration of lack of money you are looking morose, sounding helpless and getting angry with life but eventually seek the service of a financial adviser and you are asked what your total worth is. If after venting all your frustrations the financial adviser discovers that though you have no money for capital but have inherited piles of gold, balls of silver, and other precious gems, what do you think the reaction will be?. Of course you will be made to realize your lack of sense of value for what you have and reassured that you really don't have any capital problem. In the same vein, it is abnormal for a believer to be stuck in the name of lack of capital in life. What you have as part of your heritage has been taken to the stock market of life and found to be of more value than those piles of gold, balls of silver, and other precious metals. Lack of capital can be said to be a lack of the right wisdom for the situation at hand. The irony is that the needed wisdom to have your own portion and attain your height is available in your inheritance obtained by Christ for you. It is your duty to search it out from the word and ask it out in prayer.

Wisdom Will Defend You

The sure form of defense against the wicked one given to mankind (Adam) in the garden at the beginning was the instruction of wisdom. Jesus equates hearing and doing to wisdom *(Matthew 7:24).* The picture we have in our mind of a tree with red apple-like fruits, a snake coiling around a tree, and an angry God pacing up and down because his subject has just disobeyed him, has removed the real lesson of events at Eden from us. The real issue was that God was giving the sure insurance of life to mankind as instruction of wisdom. God did not tell Adam about the devil or demons nor did he tell him how hardship would feel if things went wrong. All that God did was give the key of wisdom to Adam and told him it was the guarantee against death, hardship or harm. Supernatural wisdom is a guarantee against natural and supernatural harm and onslaught of the wicked.

...but he who has been born of God keeps himself, and the wicked one does not touch him...1 John 5:18b

The devil was not presented as a strong or powerful personality on earth in the Bible. He was presented from the onset as a wile-some, cunning fellow determined to destroy. There is a place of power in the kingdom, but daily victorious living is by supernatural wisdom. It takes light, not power, to chase darkness out. For instance, the high-tension cable used in transmitting electricity carries enormous power of many watts, but as powerful as it is, it is of no use at night or in darkness unless the power is channeled into a bulb or fluorescent tube to give light. I remember growing up in a part of the world where consistent generation and distribution of electricity for the people by the government was almost an impossible task. At every opportunity, the president or a government official would come and blow big speeches on how many "megawatts" of power they were generating. But the people were never impressed. All they wanted was light to attend to the darkness of night. The speeches were thus summarized in one word - "failure." Wisdom is the light of life for saints.

The word of God is the lamp that gives the light of life. Reading or quoting of the word is not light. The entrance is what gives light. In essence, someone can read the Bible and know theology but still lack light. The entrance means the influence exerted on your inside which eventually determines your action and reaction on the outside. God as a father is more impressed with you living in safety than running into trouble to be rescued all the time. The wicked mindset of human about leadership is to run into trouble then keep running back to them for help and so establish perpetual dependence. God is too secure for that. He wants you to dwell in victory and safety and thus glorify him in liberty. He would rather you were not sick, even though he will heal you if you fall sick. He would rather you were not broke, even though he will drop manna as a rescue meal. Most of the time, God's power is given to rescue people from crisis but God's wisdom is given to keep you from crisis all together.

Wisdom Will Bring the Star in You Out

Whenever inheritance is bequeathed to an heir, it is done so that the one who inherits may use it as a launching pad to succeed in life. The same is true here. The inheritance of wisdom was given to you so that the star in you may come out to the glory of God the father. There is the know-how needed for each star to shine. There is a circuit ordained, for your shining; competition, and perspiration will not take you there. It takes the wisdom of God at work in you. One of the principal things that make people shine as star is for them to locate their own place or circuit in life. For some, it is by happenstance. Some were guided by others, but for you the wisdom of God can lead you there. For instance, not everyone will be sport stars born to coaching parents who would drive and push them to stardom. Neither will all tumble by sheer happenstance into their lot in life. For many and the majority, for that matter, what is required is a deliberate discovery, a deliberate pursuit and a deliberate delivery of the star in you. Knowing what to do, how to do it, and doing it is wisdom.

Who is like a wise man? And who knows the interpretation of a thing? A man's wisdom makes his face shine, and the sternness of his face is changed... Ecclesiastes 8:1.

Real stardom and status change in the kingdom is a product of wisdom discovered and applied.

Those who are wise shall shine like the brightness of the firmament, and those who turn many to righteousness like the stars forever and ever... Daniel 12:3.

Everlasting stardom is what wisdom confers. The world has seen many who rose like stars but fell and died like sand. For you, it is different. Shining is ever brighter, your shine is never ending; shining is forever even after departing the earth into eternity.

Chapter 5

And Even Much More

Then I looked, and I heard the voice of many angels around the throne, the living creatures, and the elders; and the number of them was ten thousand times ten thousand, and thousands of thousands, saying with a loud voice: Worthy is the Lamb who was slain to receive <u>power</u> and <u>riches</u> and <u>wisdom</u>, and <u>strength</u> and <u>honor</u> and <u>glory</u> and <u>blessing</u>!...Revelations 5:11-12.

The Heritage of Strength

You may be asking what do I need strength for as part of my inheritance, but if you didn't need it, the Lord wouldn't have packed it in your luggage. The strength as it relates to your inheritance is twofold: your outer man strength and your inner man strength.

Outer Man Strength for Assignment

You need this for your assignment here on earth so as not to be worn out before completion. The idea of success many have in their head is making plenty of money and getting banished to an island where they can sleep all day and night long doing nothing but waking up to eat and drink. This is what you do in the grave after death, except for the eating and drinking probably. But you are a living creature kept alive on earth by God to fulfill and accomplish an assignment. The only reason you are still here is because you are the light of the world and no one lights a candle and sets it idly under the bed but it is set on the candle stick against all the odds of gravity to do the work of giving light to many. Even though you are a spirit on a spiritual assignment, you still need an earth-compatible body to carry you around here on earth. Paul the apostle said that many folks in the Corinth Church could not see the link between spiritual correctness and strength of the physical body. So many of them abused the communion table and were said to be weak. They were weak physically even though they were still speaking in tongues and prophesying, but the working and vitality of their bodies were compromised and so they died prematurely. There is a law called the law of sin and death through which sickness and disease exploit the human body making it weak and or even die. You don't have to commit sin to trigger it. It was triggered by the sin in Adam. That is why it is the law of sin (singular) and death and not the law of sins (plural-which are acts of lawlessness people commit) and death. Germs were not harmful until the law of sin and death was triggered by Adam. There were no free radicals to cause sickness nor were there genetic anomalies until that law of sin and death was triggered and progressively took root in broader dimensions and varieties over the ages. This was why it sounds incredible to read of patriarchs living hundreds of years in the Bible because the overall devastating effect of the law of sin and death was progressive. Thus Adam didn't drop dead immediately when he sinned. It was the law triggered by sin that allows and enhances anything that will ultimately lead to physical death because of the spiritual death already procured for mankind. To help sustain you while you are still here on earth, Christ initiated the law of spirit of life on your behalf. It is based on this law that says that the spirit of him that raised Christ from the dead will quicken (vitalize or strengthen) your mortal body when attacked by sickness and weakness.

This sounds weird, you say. It is normal to be weak and fall sick as a human, you will say. Yes, I agree with you. It is normal to be weak, sick, and broken down, just like it is normal for humans to be born of humans. But how normal is it for humans to be born of God (born again), of course abnormal in every sense of it. A born again person should stop settling for normal and go for the supernatural and the peculiars. I would rather be weird and be healthy than be normal and grounded. There is nothing normal or sensible to the natural mind in the things of the spirit.

And if the Spirit of Him Who raised up Jesus from the dead dwells in you, [then] He Who raised up Christ Jesus from the dead will also restore to life your mortal (short-lived, perishable) bodies

through His Spirit Who dwells in you...Romans 8:11(Amp).

Inner Man Strength for Triumph

If you faint in the day of adversity, your strength is small...Proverbs 24:10

Anytime I read this scripture, I remember Darwin and pity the poor old man. This reality confused him about life so much that he eventually misunderstood the survival of the fittest concept and took solace in atheism. I wish he had seen the light that survival is truly for the fittest and so Christ gave us strength as part of our inheritance to not just survive but thrive and be the fittest! On earth, there is always a day called the day of adversity, which may be plenty, may last for long, may be repeated often and can even be very painful or make you cry. No wonder the word did not say if you cry in the day of adversity, your strength is small. You can cry and throw tantrums, but don't ever give up. If it were pleasant, it wouldn't be called the day of adversity, but the good news is you don't have to cave in or fail in such a day. Your adversary, the devil, is the one behind the day of adversity. The light here is that his strength is measurable or can be quantified unlike God who is omnipotent. What you don't need in such a day, if you want to win, is small strength. You need much strength to thrive against all odds.

What sort of strength?

Inner man strength or strength from your inside is the requisite for triumph when the chips are down.

Well-built muscle and well-groomed bodies are as good as useless in the day of adversity. As good as university degrees are, they don't hold in the day of adversity. Part of your inheritance is the entitlement to be strengthened from the inside when in an adverse situation. You don't have to start sounding and feeling helpless. Quit yourself and stand strong immovable, knowing well that you have strength in the reserve to cope and go through all the way.

Therefore I ask that you do not lose heart at my tribulations for you, which is your glory. For this reason I bow my knees to the Father of our Lord Jesus Christ, from whom the whole family in heaven and earth is named, that He would grant you, according to the riches of His glory, to be strengthened with might through His Spirit in the inner man...Ephesians 3:13-16.

What if I am fainting already, you ask. That is not a problem. Just wait on the Lord and he will renew your strength from the unending reserve of your inheritance of strength. In one of my books I said prayer is not a show of strength but a channel to acquire the strength you lack. How did Paul go about this business of strength so that the saints will not faint because of adversity? By bowing his knees in prayer. When you can't do anything again, pray. Know full well that God will grant you enough strength to prevail. Never must you give up. There is strength in your inheritance and you can take on any adverse situation and not faint or cave in.

The Heritage of Honor

You have been honored by God. You don't go out of your way to seek the same from men again, because it is just a matter of time before you will walk in the full account of your inheritance. Honor must follow you, even from the worst beast. Honor was placed on man at creation to establish his dominion in the realm of all living. This was why the lion could not harm him. Honor placed all things under his feet.

What is man that you are mindful of him, and the son of man that you visit him? For you have made him a little lower than the angels, and you have crowned him with glory and honor. You have made him to have dominion over the works of your hands; you have put all things under his feet... Psalms 8:4-6.

My sanctified guess is that this statement was not made by a man, but that David overheard another kind of creation say it to God in worship while he was fellowshipping with God. David could not forget what he heard and had to say it eventually because of the profoundness. Likely it was an animal or angel or other creation who was saying it and a man of the spirit just caught the revelation and wrote it down in his spirit. You remember the same David overheard the Lord saying unto my Lord on another occasion to sit at his right hand till he made his enemy his foot stool. In the earlier case above, the dominion of mankind over flying and creeping creatures was traced to the honor bestowed by God, lost by Adam, but now restored through Christ as an inheritance of the saints. This is very important because many believers still fear people who through diabolical means can operate through flying, creeping, or swimming animals to hurt or harm others. In your case, you are the man or woman in charge. Your honor puts all witches, wizards, occultists, diabolical and hurtful beasts under your dominion. You should go about life with an innate sense of honor that you are too dignified to be molested or harassed. Anything or anyone who dares it does so at a great cost that you must inflict through the sword of your mouth. The world is full of beastly beings. Paul wrestled with some in Ephesus, but he prevailed. You are honored to prevail among all the living, no matter how wicked they may be. The truth is they don't have to like you. They just need to fall in line while you are present - no inferiority complex for you again! The revelation of this truth can reinforce your heritage of exemption in the face of disaster, whether natural or manmade. You can sleep and be at rest in darkness without any fear of being harmed. There is an aura of honor around you. You must be conscious of and keep reinforcing it by believing it and declaring just as the psalmist did. This was one of the secrets behind David slaying of bear, lion, and eventually Goliath. You can slay all things, too. You are too honored to be the victim.

The Heritage of Glory

Grace and peace be multiplied to you in the knowledge of God and of Jesus our Lord, as His divine power has given to us all things that pertain to life and godliness, through the knowledge of Him who called us to glory and virtue, 2 Peter 1:2-3 (KJV).

The Christian call is not a call unto failure in life. It is not a call unto mediocrity but unto glory and excellence. The out-radiance of divine essence on Earth is part and parcel of Christian heritage. Christ, the last Adam, came to raise mankind up unto what we fell short of in the first Adam, which is the glory of God. With this at the back of our mind, you approach life not as a trial at success but as someone who will succeed no matter what. You must approach assignments as one who has what it takes to succeed. You might have to learn more. You might have to burn the so-called night candle like Peter on the sea, but you can bet your life on it that at the end of the day you will come out a success. You might even experience some initial setbacks that can be seen as failure, but it is never over until your net is full of fishes. For many reasons, including being in the wrong place and doing the wrong things, a Christian might encounter a temporary failure or set back in one area of life or the other. At the end of the day, you must still succeed, getting your path right and making appreciable progress. Failing in one area or at one stage or the other does not interpret to eventual failure for a believer. Even if you fail in many things, you will eventually succeed in one thing that will dwarf your initial failure, heal you initial wound, and culminate in absolute fulfillment in your race of life. No matter how much you have gone down, there is still glory in your calling and laid up in your inheritance. Search it out.

You can never go down and short of glory as a Christian more than you did as an unbeliever. At that phase of life, all have sinned and come short of the glory of God no matter how high they seem to have risen in the eyes of the world. Now that you are raised with Christ, the real you dwells in the place of success with Christ. To be called into glory necessarily does not mean to be called into fivefold ministry such as a pastor. A pastoral calling is not a cheap way out of life. I grew up in a society where all uncalled men and women were pastors, prophets, and apostles simply because they had seen and desired to be like a few who were genuinely called into such offices, who pursued their calling faithfully and were elevated to societal prominence with outward success by God. As a result, many shallow, uncalled men and women simply desiring filty lucre are all over the place eking a living by polluting and mucking up the sacred water and altar of fivefold ministry.

The reality is that no believer needs to be a pastor to succeed. All that is needed is to discover your own place of calling whether in the ministry or industry, search out your inheritance therein, and appropriate same for unlimited glory. Part of what Christ got for you as an inheritance is glory, even the out-radiance of divine essence in what you are called to be and manifest. This is the only way the Josephs, Daniels, Shadrachs, Meshachs, Abednegos, Esthers, Obedidums, and many more successful kingdom representatives in the market place of this dark world of today can emerge. Of what gain would it be to God as a father if all his children were fetchers of waters and hewers of wood to the heathen. The irony is that many Christians are seeking the glory of their destiny from the World whereas Jesus said all they can get from the world is tribulations. When the world presents all it has got as glory, believers gets intimidated and frustrated many times, giving up on themselves and settling down for whatever comes their way by conformity. Good news is that behind the veil of the challenges (tribulations) the world brings is the out radiance of the glory of saints, so Jesus said you should be of good cheer. The world necessarily did not like Daniel, Joseph, and Esther in their days, but they needed them. By the virtue of inheritance, you matter to your generation. The world needs you more than you think. Lift your head up and lend a helping hand to the dark and dying world.

The glory is eternal. Whatever we see of this out-radiance of divine essence here is just the tip of an iceberg. Full manifestation cannot be fathomed now until we enter eternity and see it ourselves. In the Old Testament, God used to give a foretaste of things to come by manifesting the glow such as was in Solomon temple and mount of transfiguration. But now we need no physical appearance of any halo as a reflection of glory and divine presence. Just like we don't need the earth to quake or building to shake like in the Act of Apostle for us to know that God has heard and answered our prayer. Outward signs are to help human unbelief when knowledge is limited. Now you are the habitation of divine presence and the reflection of His glory. You are the partaker of his glorious inheritance not a shameful ignominy and dreg of the society. Reading glossy magazines full of glossy stories and glossed personalities must not derail you into an inferiority complex of any kind so as to depart from the living God. Many of them glitter outside but are miserable inside. You are the only one who has it going within and without.

The Heritage of Blessing

Blessing is the divine empowerment to be fruitful, multiply, replenish, and have dominion.

And God blessed them, and God said unto them, be fruitful, and multiply, and replenish the earth, and subdue it: and have dominion over the fish of the sea, and over the fowl of the air, and over every living thing that moves upon the earth (KJV)... Genesis 1:28.

The whole concept of blessing is clearly shown here. Blessing was God's idea. No one saw the need and prayed for it. It was God who deemed it fit for man to have blessing upon his life. At this point, you need to bear it in mind that Adam (mankind) had a whole city or garden in the east of Eden unto himself. He had food, shelter, gold, and all material provisions he needed even before he was formed. So the concept of blessing is beyond the shallow pursuit of necessities and material gain. The blessing of the Lord is not money but can make you rich financially when well appropriated. The blessing is not a car or house but can empower you to have your transportation and shelter needs well met and much more. When the blessing of the Lord finds physical or material manifestations in your hand we colloquially refer to them as blessings (plural), which are the byproduct of the real empowerment, even the blessing. You are too loaded to be pursuing the byproduct when the source is in your kingdom inheritance. This was what Jesus meant when he said seek first the kingdom of God and all these things shall flow your way as by products. When you are truly and genuinely interested in and pursuing the blessing or empowerment in your inheritance for fruitfulness, multiplication, and dominion here on earth, material prosperity or a safe journey of destiny is inevitable.

Be Fruitful

To be fruitful means to bear results, to end up better than where you start, to gain size and speed, to cover distance in the journey of destiny. When you hear of fruit, the first thing that should come into your mind is seeding. To be fruitful you need to see yourself a seed ready to be sown for productivity. You don't just spend your life, you invest your life. You don't just spend your time and resources; you sow your time and resources as seed of development with expectation of tangible return. When you understand this, whatever you are going through now will be seen as a seeding of sort, ready to yield unto you the peaceable fruit of righteousness. Paul the apostle got this concept right so much that he rated what looked like unbearable suffering as light affliction. Not an affliction for sake of affliction, not an affliction in order to just suffer, not an affliction to destroy them or to make them look like a saint. The affliction was seen as seed time working out something for them, even the fruit of eternal glory.

Therefore we do not lose heart. Even though our outward man is perishing, yet the inward man is being renewed day by day. For our light affliction, which is but for a moment, is working for us a far more exceeding and eternal weight of glory, while we do not look at the things which are seen, but at the things which are not seen? For the things which are seen are temporary, but the things which are not seen are eternal...2 Corinthians 4: 16-18.

Good farmers will tell you that once they sow their seed in the soil, they let go of it to the soil. They don't go there digging up and checking on the seed to see if it will succeed. They don't go there crying on the seed because it is getting rotten and losing color. They let go with expectation. The expectation is what makes them water their seed and dress the field. The same expectation makes them go back there in harvest to reap with a sickle. This is the real deal. To be fruitful, you cannot focus on what is going wrong and what is painful and what is not working and challenging in your life. Sufficient for the day is the evil thereof. So if you want to focus on the evil, your hand will be full unto the overflowing. But sufficient for the day is also the opportunity thereof. As a fruitful one, you will need to focus on the unseen opportunities and provisions in your inheritance at the expense of the seen challenges with expectations. What happens once you do that is the disappearing of the challenges since they are temporal and the appearance of the fruits since they are eternal. The good news is, you are blessed or empowered to bear fruit as a seed. The blessing is in your inheritance in Christ. You are energized to have results, to end up better than you are now, to gain size and gather speed for better arrival. It is in your inheritance.

Multiply

Increase is the ordained way to true greatness in God's kingdom. This was why God did not create 10 billion people in the beginning. All he created was one and put the empowerment to increase to several billions in them. The same principle was employed in bringing many sons unto glory. All that was needed was just a captain of salvation, one Lord, even Christ Jesus. Increase is not a Harvard or Oxford but kingdom-postulated theory. In your own case, you have an inheritance in which is the empowerment to increase to your dream size. Increase is not alien to your heritage. It is not what you run from pillar to post for. It is there as part of your inheritance of blessing. Once you can see this, no matter the size of that business in your hand, you will not be intimidated or jealous of bigger ones but give God thanks knowing fully that in your own inheritance is the empowerment for multiplication, which is a faster and more accelerated way to increase.

Listen to me, you who follow after righteousness, you who seek the LORD: look to the rock from which you were hewn, and to the hole of the pit from which you were dug. Look to Abraham your father, and to Sarah who bore you; for I called him alone, and blessed him and increased him. For the LORD will comfort Zion, he will comfort all her waste places; he will make her wilderness like Eden, and her desert like the garden of the LORD; joy and gladness will be found in it, thanksgiving and the voice of melody.........Isaiah 51: 1-3

There is growth reserved for you. No matter how small you start, it is inherent in your inheritance of blessing to multiply. You may boldly declare that your beginning might be small but shall greatly increase. It will happen by the blessing of inheritance.

Replenish

Renewal and continuity is what kept the earth through ages and generation once it was initiated in Eden. The power to do so is the power of blessing. After the flood, God had to bless the last man standing, even Noah to ensure the same continuity. It is not in God's will for good things to start and finish in your lineage with you. Your posterity matters to God as much as your prosperity and so he releases in you the blessing to perpetuate or renew your lineage. When the same blessing came on Abraham, it went all the way through the ages even unto us, which Abraham knew not in flesh but through Christ. Understanding this mystery can bring your wayward child back home to the way of light. That you are blessed for continuity, renewal, and replenishing means there must always be a head or heads upon which blessing must rest in your lineage. Jacob was crooked from the womb. This empowerment of blessing in Isaac straightened him up in the process of time and he became the prince he was meant to be. There might be medical conditions that prevent you from having babies as you desire. The creative and re-creative miracle necessary for reproduction or replenishing your lineage in God is resident in your inheritance. You can set the medical report aside now and face the reality of your godly inheritance of blessing to replenish. When this light glows in your heart, it will lighten your body and banish barrenness. I see bareness banished from your womb. I see infertility terminated in you and your children come forth now in the mighty name of Jesus Christ, amen.

Subdue and Dominate

There is no neutral ground here on earth. It is either you subdue or be subdued, dominate or be dominated.

It is in your inheritance of blessing to subdue and dominate in your territory not manipulate others in their territory. It is part of your inheritance to be unstoppable on your tract, no matter the height and the size of what you are confronted with. You can now see who is going down in the battle you are fighting; the opposition, of course. You are empowered to cut issues and forces that be to size and level all hindrances on your path. It is part of the empowerment of blessing in your inheritance not to be put under no matter what. You can't afford the "masses' mentality". You are not part of the masses. You are a peculiar people, not to be pitied by any chance but to be envied, feared, and revered by all means. God said your fear shall be on all the beastly creations and not the other way round. Dominion is too inherent in your inheritance for you to be a weakling.

Yinka Akintunde

Chapter 6

Partaker Not Spectator

Even though Christ got the inheritance for us already, the value is only delivered to partakers, not spectators or commentators. Just as Christ died for salvation and yet many still die unsaved, so can many live in the kingdom as strugglers roaming and hustling with no kingdom backup for their life. Your case is different from this point onward. My assignment is not just to paint a picture of the inheritance unto you but to call you to the table, if you are not yet there, and if you are there, to urge you to dig deeper than ever before. There are three platforms upon which you qualify for all we have been discussing as inheritance heretofore.

Mankind platform

Reading our anchor verses for the last two chapters from the book of Revelation, we found the full list of what Christ obtained for us. A religious mind averse to saints living well and good can quickly say, "oh no, Christ did it for the angels or the natural Jews or for himself." Well, a proper look at the preceding verses will clearly show us who the subject matter of inheritance was focused on.

And I saw in the right hand of him that sat on the throne a book written within and on the backside, sealed with seven seals. And I saw a strong angel proclaiming with a loud voice, who is worthy to open the book, and to lose the seals thereof? And no man in heaven, or in earth, neither under the earth, was able to open the book, neither to look thereon. And I wept much, because no man was found worthy to open and to read the book, neither to look thereon. And one of the elders said unto me, Weep not: behold, the Lion of the tribe of Judah, the Root of David, hath prevailed to open the book, and to loose the seven seals thereof. And I beheld, and, lo, in the midst of the throne and of the four beasts, and in the midst of the elders, stood a Lamb as it had been slain, having seven horns and seven eyes, which are the seven Spirits of God sent forth into all the earth...Revelation 5:1-6 (KJV).

The scroll or the book that contained the mystery of the testament to the inheritance was sealed. They needed a man and not just anyone to open it because the content is meant for men. The rendering in other versions of the Bible said, "no one was found" but the KJV states it clearly. They were not looking for just anyone but for any man. This was why when they wanted to describe the one who opened it; they didn't call him Alpha and Omega or son of God. His root in man was what they emphasized here in describing him and not his divinity. In fact, he sat on the throne as a lamb (slain and risen as man for man), not as the Lord.

We can see a clear allegory between lamb and man in what happened to Abraham when he was called to offer Isaac. A lamb was eventually used in the place of the man Isaac the moment Abraham's obedience was complete and ratified. Christ as a man completed the journey of obedience and was offered on the cross as a man, but in the court of heaven he was seen as lamb that was slain for men in the place of man. As you can see, once the seal of inheritance was opened, the seven spirits of God, which represent the full spirit of God we refer to as the Holy Spirit, were not sent to all the Heaven but all the earth to see to the administration of the purchased inheritance, hallelujah!

He was not sent to Israel or America. He was sent to all the earth, geographical locations, and nationalities then became irrelevant and inconsequential in the issue of kingdom inheritance. Anyone can go as far as he or she can see no matter where you are from. Significant is the fact that they searched all the gurus, prophets (first and the last), deities dead and living (in heaven and the earth), but no one was found worthy to undertake the task. They searched all of African deities, Asian deities, Greek and Roman gods and goddesses. They must have searched among the human rights activists too, and the free thinkers and the philosophers but no one was found worthy but Jesus Christ, the son of God who became the son of man so that the sons of men might become the sons of God.

As a human being, you have fulfilled the first criteria of qualification for the godly inheritance. The inheritance is not for dogs, cats, and other pets. It is not for alien, angels, or demons. It is for mankind.

God-kind platform

Once the son of God became the son of man and died for man, the exchange was complete. The road was opened eternally for us, the sons of men, to be empowered to become sons of God. Having received Christ through new birth, you are now a son of God, no matter your gender. The new creation is not the flesh but is housed in the flesh, which could be male or female. The inheritance distribution knows no gender boundary. You can have and become as much as you will in God's will and purpose for your life irrespective of your gender. The inheritance originated from God who is now your father. You are not an alien again but a fellow citizen in the household of God. This understanding will erase the beggarly mindset from you forever. You are not trying to persuade a very difficult and stingy God to have mercy on you, a worthless worm, no! You are simply lining up for your own lot and portion of your father's wealth. You are not trying to nick what belongs to the world with apology and fear of being harassed or misunderstood. You are boldly laying claim to your father's property with understanding. Once you are born again, you become a God-kind, you are sourced from God, your substance emanates from him, and you are an offshoot of divinity living in human flesh now. This is why am not ashamed to preach and live prosperity, glory to God!

Christ-kind platform

The best and ultimate way to describe you is as a Christ kind, the one who has divinity in flesh. You are part and parcel of Christ, so we are called the body of Christ, member in particular, Jesus Christ being the head. You are mixed together with Christ, an inseparable entity, what he has you have, what he won, you have won, what he inherited, you also have inherited.

The Spirit itself bears witness with our spirit, that we are the children of God: And if children, then heirs; heirs of God, and joint-heirs with Christ; if so be that we suffer with him, that we may be also glorified together. For I reckon that the sufferings of this present time are not worthy to be compared with the glory which shall be revealed in us. For the earnest expectation of the creature waits for the manifestation of the sons of God...Romans 8:16-19 (KJV).

Remember it was the same Spirit that was revealed as the seven spirits of God earlier on and sent into the earth. Now this is part of what he was sent to do. He was sent to bear witness in you of your sonship to God, your heirship in God, and your joint heirship with Christ. You cannot be an heir to nothing. It must be to an inheritance.

I deliberately showed you the verses that follow because I have heard many saints who are comfortable with the preaching of the suffering, but once we talk of the glory or blessing that follows, they are angry. They call it wealth and health gospel. Well, what is wrong with wealth and health? Who in their right mind does not want either? They agree saints can be sick, but to be healed, no way. They are comfortable with saints being the messenger, but to be the manager, no way. When you show them verses like the one above that whatever a saint goes through God wants to turn it around for glory or breakthrough, yeah, but the glory is in heaven, they say. How wrong this is. Verse 19 started as continuity of the preceding verse hence the word "for" which means "because." So, because of the turnaround or the breakthrough to the challenges or suffering, the whole creation is waiting for the manifestation of the glory of that breakthrough or blessings. If the glory is just in heaven, why should the whole creation be waiting for it here on earth? We all know that the whole creation is not going to heaven unless they are born again. But why are they waiting? They are waiting because they are suffering, too. They have challenges, too. Challenges are not peculiar to Christians. They want us to lead the triumph train and show the way out. The solutions to all challenges and suffering are rooted in the inheritance of the saints. No wonder the beloved wept much when no man was found worthy to lose the seal of the inheritance carrying the solutions to all humanity's challenges.

Furthermore, because we are united with Christ, we have received an inheritance from God, for he chose us in advance, and he makes everything work out according to his plan...Ephesians 1:11 (NLT).

Your brother won the contest. He is the champion, and he got the inheritance, so you can partake in the glory. Can you beat that, awesome!

You need a Paul

In the anchor verses for chapter one of this book, Acts 26:18, Paul clearly defined his mission and commission, which was to open the people's eyes of understanding, turn them from darkness of confusion and ignorance to light of certainty, and to bring them under divine influence, which would put them in the receiving position for their inheritance. What a pastor that was, what a leader! A man who was not just collecting and manipulating people for gain, a man who was set to help them lay hold of their own lot in life. He was not even turning them to himself, but unto God. He was determined to see men get what they ought to get and be what they ought to be in God. He was a good shepherd, leading and guiding the sheep to the place of brooks and pastures. He wasn't busy thinking about how much milk and fur he could glean out of them.

For I have not shunned to declare to you the whole counsel of God...Act 20:27

This was what leaders are sent to do in church, to help you see the whole counsel of God per time, so you can line up with it. God is not stupid to have called your leader to that place of leadership to declare unto you his planned purpose and counsel. If you are his mouth piece to the Church, he would have called and chosen you rather than the pastor you are under now. Anytime you have outgrown being a sheep in a flock under your pastor, leave rather than injuring yourself and the body of Christ through rebellion.

And I will give you shepherds according to my heart, who will feed you with knowledge and understanding...Jeremiah 3:15.

Pastors are not manipulators but feeder of flocks with knowledge and understanding. Pastors are not mere friends and colleagues of the flocks but appointed feeders. We are all God's children and equal in our stand of salvation before God as his children, but God has appointed some as pastors and given the task of feeding you with the knowledge and understanding that will help you partake of your own inheritance. God knows you are educated, old, experienced, and well exposed, but there is a pastor who fills your size and purpose, such will God appoint to you for feeding. Once you get to a stage where you can never stay nor feed under any pastor again, there is a big problem. You need a pastor; you need a leader who will illuminate you by the word of God so that you can partake of your own inheritance. You can never outgrow the sheep status in the kingdom. You can never be too educated to be a sheep in the kingdom. Once you can't be taught and can't be turned by the word of God through your leader, forget about inheritance.

A little success and a few lifting in life have made a lot of saints lose their lofty inheritance. Once money shows up with a few degrees, many can be unteachable and argumentative to their own peril. The Berea brethren were not noble because they were argumentative, insubordinate, rebellious, and fighting their leaders. They attained nobility because they <u>readily received</u> the word of God <u>with all readiness of mind</u> and were studious enough to <u>search the scriptures</u> if what they have received were so. ***Acts 17:10-11.*** What of if it were not so? They would have discarded it and follow the truth because that was all they wanted to know, not an argument of superiority of knowledge or a fight of being right while others are wrong. The effects of their attitude led to a growth in their faith and conversion of others to the body, not the scattering of the Church and the backsliding of others. ***Acts 17: 12***

<u>Paul Will Need To Leave.</u>

For the inheritance to come, Paul had to leave one way or the other. He had preached to them, taught them, laid hands on them, visited them, and even organised welfare for the ones in acute need. But as far as inheritance was concerned, that was as far he could go as a pastor. In as much as God had sent pastors and ministry gifts to the body of Christ to help build you up, no one can take you into your inheritance but you. It takes personal responsibility to eat the fruit of the land. Moses might part the Red Sea and Joshua part Jordan. Once in Canaan, each man had to plant a vineyard, water, and harvest it. It is a land where the choice of digging brass is left in your hand. The mentality of absolute dependence is not Christianity but another form of slavery. Running to a seer to see visions for you, tell you to travel or not, show you your husband, read your future in a crystal ball, chose a mate for you among many photographs you brought is the short cut to slavery after salvation. Inheritance belongs to the free born, not the bound slave.

No matter how much your pastor cares about and prays for you, he can only show you the way. You have to make the journey by yourself into your inheritance. I love my son, but I can't train as a doctor on his behalf. Many leaders love the dependence so much it gives them a sense of worth, while many followers also see it as sign of being loved by their leader. It is a sign of not growing and inheritance is for sons who by reason of use have been exercising their spiritual senses and muscles to take charge of life. Paul loved the Ephesians saints so much that he bowed his knee to God on their behalf all the time, but that is as much as he could do. He still had to commend them to God and the word of grace, which they would lay hold of by themselves before they could be qualified for their own lot of inheritance.

You need inspiration, encouragement, enlightenment, and empowerment through your leaders, but you can only see through their lights. You shine by your own light, and inheritance is about shining. Arise and shine means you must take responsibility, because your light, not your pastor's light, has come. Your pastor's light is to enlighten you so you can see to the coming of your own light, which is the only light you can shine with. "Our" inheritance is different from "your own" inheritance. When they got Canaan as a land, each of them occupied his own lot and had personal exploits there. Even though they divided it according to tribes, families, and lineages, it still eventually got broken down to individual lots. This is the reason why the quantum of anointing in the church you attend is not what finally determines your lot but what you do with it. Many people are jumping from church to church looking for the moves and the trends and the special anointing that will fix them up. Twenty years later, the jumping around journey is still ongoing. They mistake congregational charismata as a replacement for personal responsibility.

Isaac inherited the blessing from Abraham, which enabled and spoke for him in the days of famine, but he still took responsibility to channel the blessing right. Abraham was a nomad rearing animals. Isaac would rather have planted crops, and he prospered that way. Though Abraham laid hands on him to bless him, it was not Abraham that heard God for him when the chips were down. In fact, Abraham was dead. It was Isaac who heard God. It was his decision to obey, and it was he who dug well and chose not to give up in the face of oppositions but sowed in the land. Glory to God, it was Isaac who reaped hundred fold, grew, became great till the Philistine envied him. It was him, not Abraham his pastor, who was given the entrance into and partaking of the Rehoboth inheritance. **Genesis 26:1-32.**

The same blessing came to Jacob, but he was the one who fought the battle of life and death for survival with an angel, not Isaac his pastor or Rebecca his Sunday school teacher! It was he who channeled the blessing into initiative in Laban's house and provoked angelic visitation for blessings and prosperity to flow through the flocks out of his inheritance of blessing. **Genesis 30:25-43.**

Thus the man became exceedingly prosperous, and had large flocks, female and male servants, and camels and donkeys...Genesis 30:43

It was the man who took responsibility who became prosperous, not just the man on whose head hands were laid.

Jesus was a compassionate, knowledgeable, caring and an anointed leader to his 12 disciples while he was here on earth. But he had to leave for them to be what they needed to be and have what they needed to have as inheritance. In specific terms, he told them that it was necessary for him to go and leave them alone to their destiny. Absolute human dependence is not God's way of evolving champions. Eagles are trained to be released into their own exploits individually. As long as the eaglet is still carried, it is not yet ready to fly neither is it set for higher heights than the carrier. God is not retrogressive. He wants the offspring to go further than their ancestors, and this is not possible as long as the heir is not left alone to develop the skeleton and muscles of life needed to triumph through the necessary bruising and using.

It Could be Lonely Here

Loneliness is not strange in the land of inheritance. In fact, you need it to lay hold of your own inheritance. Loneliness may not mean you are living alone in the bush like a leper or monk, but even in the midst of multitudes, personal dealings are inevitable. Don't be anxious if you feel lonely, if you are misunderstood, or if no one comes along. You are not out for "our" inheritance. You are out for your own inheritance. Abraham was called and commanded into an alone world as we saw earlier. What he could not do by himself, Lot's departure, was personally orchestrated by God. The moment Lot left and Abraham was feeling bad for family ties thinking of how his father and brother would be feeling in heaven about the whole issue, God showed up to say, *"I know about it, now lift up your eyes and see your own inheritance."*

How come we didn't hear of Isaac's uncles, cousins, in-laws, and friends when there was famine, or do you think he didn't have any? They were not principal actors so they were not mentioned. They may have done good things in his life, but God chose not to mention them so you can learn that in the journey of your own inheritance, you are the principal actor. The action and inaction, the outcome is left for and to you and not to others no matter how close they are to you.

No one can enter massive things in God while tied to aprons of sentiment and unnecessary attachments. Jacob was pushed out of the house with nothing but the blessing. Esau got all Isaac's material wealth. No one is proud to be Esau's descendant today. Jacob was alone with Laban. God saw to it that Laban was never nice like an uncle to Jacob. He dealt with him purely on business term, a difficult one, for that matter. Which uncle will ask you to be serving 14 years for wives and six years for free and yet chasing you all over the bush because you got blessed afterward? Remember Joseph, David, and even Jesus -these were men who felt the pain of loneliness at the point of birth of their destiny. Jesus could not hide his own, so he cried, *Eloi Eloi Lama Sabachthani.* Thank God they all went through it and came out with their own inheritance. Joseph became a preserver, David became the father of the Lord, and Jesus inherited a better name than angels that at the name he inherited every knee must bow and tongue confess that He is the lord to the glory of God the father. It may be lonely, but you shall get there no matter what.

Having a clear understanding of what your inheritance entails and your platform of access. It is necessary for us to see what to do in order to lay hold of same. This shall be our focus in the next chapters.

Yinka Akintunde

CHAPTER 7

THE WORD OF INHERITANCE

So now, brethren, I commend you to God and to the word of His grace, which is able to build you up and give you an inheritance among all those who are sanctified...Acts 20:32.

The oneness between God and his word was highlighted here when both God and his word are referred to as a singular entity: which "is" able to build you up to the right stature of the spirit needed for the manifestations of what had been given you already. When God wants to do anything on earth, he does not jump down and start running around. What he does is reveal his mind and intent through his word. The same word will be incubated upon by his spirit as seed to hatch the desired effect. When God wanted to recreate the chaotic, dark, and empty world in the book of Genesis, he didn't jump down. We were not even told if he was sitting or standing while working on his creation. All we were told was that he released his spirit and his word for effects that are still not deniable. It was not a coincidence that the Bible started from that point. God could have inspired it to be given or written in another way and still achieve his purpose. The reason the whole revelation of divine intervention on earth was revealed to us as it was in Genesis chapter one is for you to be able to see and imitate divine pattern whenever you want to see God's hand build or change anything here on earth. There is no point mourning the undesirable you meet on ground. God, from the beginning, has shown us what to do to impose the "desired" you want to see on the "undesirable" you are sick and tired of seeing.

<u>The Concept or Logos of God</u>

I am not trying to intimidate with semantics here, but trying to help you appreciate what you are dealing with as the word of God. The first and foundational form in which God's word will come to you is what we call logos, which means the concept or the idea in the mind of God. The Bible, for instance, is given by the inspiration of the spirit as God's concept of what are his plan, purpose, promises, and provisions for us as his children. In the logos are many instances of people of different backgrounds from different nations under different circumstance who related with God in the past. The idea is not to clone such people out of you but for you to see God's perfect way of going about life if you find yourself under similar circumstances.

For instance in Acts 8:26-40, there was a eunuch from Ethiopia who was saved by listening to the gospel in clear terms for the first time even though he had been a religious man before. The take is this - suppose you want to be saved. You don't need to tick all the boxes like the eunuch. I mean you don't have to be from Ethiopia, or be an eunuch (a celibate). You don't need to be sitting in a carriage as he was and have a Philip transported to you by the vehicle of the spirit and go through the same process as the eunuch did in order to be saved. Even though the whole text is the word of God, but the concept or the idea, which is the mind of God, communicated to us there is that anybody can be saved anywhere if they believe in Jesus and confess him with their mouth. Sarah got Isaac at the age of 90 but the idea or concept is not that you should be 90 to get yours but the mind of God is that it can never be too late for you. The written word is given to us as the logos or the concept and idea of what the mind of God is on every issue. Therefore, the logos become our sole and ultimate standard; it is our final reference point concerning the will and mind of God as his children.

Many other books such as this one you are reading are inspired to help you interpret the logos and show you the mind of God in a broken down, easily digestible form as it relates to you today. The preaching and the teachings you listen to are also in this class, communicating the mind or concept of God to you. That is why you can be listening to word about healing not because you are sick or want to be healed of a sickness but to entrench the mind of God in your mind concerning health and well-being. The Bible is the fountain and foundation upon which any other word must stand no matter who is saying it. We cannot build Christianity upon the Bible and new age books or Quran or seven books of Moses or any other form of books whatsoever. I have heard Christians bringing out other gospels from one "saint" and or guru claiming they are as good as the Bible and thus must be considered in the stake of things as a Christian. This is the deceit of the devil. The Bible is **the given word** not one of the given words for Christians as the revelation of the mind of God, **2 Timothy 3:16**. In a nutshell, what is the relevance of the logos or the word of God in your journey of inheritance as a map? In this case, we mean first of all the Bible, and then other inspired literatures, inspired teachings and Preachings.

(i) The word is the mind of God

The first thing you need is to be aware of the way God thinks, the way he sees things, so as to know the way he wants you to think and see things, too. God said his ways are not man's way neither is his thought man's thought. How then can we reconcile the two opposing paradigms seeing that two cannot work together unless they eventually agree? God being the senior partner in the journey of inheritance will have to reveal his mind to us and the sure way he does this is by his word. Not to know the mind of God is not humility, it is ignorance.

For My thoughts are not your thoughts, nor are your ways my ways," says the LORD. For as the heavens are higher than the earth, so are my ways higher

than your ways, and my thoughts than your thoughts. Isaiah 55:8.

When it comes to the mind of God on issues of life, God said this is the picture and Christians love quoting it as a way of escaping responsibility of knowing. But God is not saying we cannot know or access his mind. He just said that his mind and ways are naturally not on the same plane as yours. God is not saying this is the whole picture. The statement doesn't ends there. The whole picture is revealed in the subsequent verses.

For as the rain comes down, and the snow from heaven, and do not return there, but water the earth, and make it bring forth and bud, that it may give seed to the sower and bread to the eater, so shall My word be that goes forth from My mouth; it shall not return to Me void, but it shall accomplish what I please, and it shall prosper in the thing for which I sent it. For you shall go out with joy, and be led out with peace...Isaiah 55:9-12a.

God said the bridge between my higher thoughts, my higher ways and your lower ones is my word, which will reveal the way to go about in peace and be led with joy unto you. The will of God, his promises, and provisions are revealed in the logos so that by them you can have hope upon which you can build your faith in love.

For whatever things were written before were written for our learning, that we through the patience and comfort of the Scriptures might have hope...Romans 15:4.

(ii) The word is the law of the spirit unto life

Life is governed and made to work by laws. The word of God reveals unto you the laws of the spirit that makes life work. When God said let there be light, he was not guessing or suggesting. He was establishing and imposing the law of the spirit upon the prevailing darkness on the earth. The word of God is not a moral law. Morality differs from place to place, and the word of God is not a set of rules given so we can formulate the constitution for democracy out of it. Doing that is good, but the purpose is way beyond that. The word of God is the revelation of the law of spirit given to regulate and rule your own world. Laws are to be observed as the statue and standard, so is the word of God. It is given for doing. The word is not for quoting or debating. It is for doing thereby bringing the doer to the place of responsibility where inheritance is entrusted. The wisdom of God comes across to you first through his word. Doing it makes you wise. For instance, **Philippians 4:6-7** shows us how to bring God on the scene of chaos. It shows us that having banished anxiety of losing out first; the next thing to do is to make your <u>request</u> known to God, not your anger or your complaints. Even when your flesh wants to do otherwise or your mind is saying something contrary, asking you what have you got to show for all your previous prayers.

Surely I have taught you statutes and judgments, just as the LORD my God commanded me that you should act according to them in the land which you go to possess. Therefore, be careful to observe them; for this is your wisdom and your understanding in the sight of the peoples who will hear all these statutes, and say, 'Surely this great nation is a wise and understanding people. For what great nation is there that has God so near to it, as the LORD our God is to us, for whatever reason we may call upon Him.......... Deuteronomy 4:5-7.

Inheritance is embedded in the covenants built upon promises. When you were not saved, you had no obligation to observe the laws that garrison the castles of the promises because you were an alien to the inside anyway, **Ephesians 2:11-12.** But now that you have come to God by Christ, the word of God is the law of the spirit that garrisons the castles of promises upon which the new covenant that bestowed the inheritance is built. When you study or listen to the logos of God, and keep meditating on it, it will recondition your internal milieu to initiate the change you desire. Your thinking pattern will start changing, so are your actions and reactions and eventually your result **Joshua1:8.**

The Rhema from the Spirit

The whole Bible as scripture contains what will make you complete. At the delivery point, the word comes to you as rhema or specific spoken word for a reason and a season. Like the pouch of a warrior with many arrows, so is the written word of God packaged for you as the will and mind of God ready for use at any point the need arises. When a particular need arises and a particular word is fired at the target for specific effect, such is called the rhema of God.

We had a challenge in the area of conception after marriage for a few years. We would have loved to start having our babies immediately after the wedding, but all efforts did not yield the desired result. We saw specialists in some of the best hospitals in London. We ran all kinds of tests. Everything was "normal" but the miscarriages continued up to number five. We were sitting down at the Whip's Cross Hospital in East London one day after my wife had an unrelated procedure, which the doctor said would even further reduce the chance of conception with no possibility at all for six months at least. I could see the tears welling up in my wife's eyes on the hospital bed. The situation had moved from bad to worse from the human perspective. Well, I turned my face away from her on the side settee and spoke in tongues quietly telling God there was a supernatural way out. Immediately, I heard the spirit of God in me say open your Bible to Romans 8:32. I knew what was there, but I opened the New Testament Bible in my hand there any way and I heard God say, "*If I can give you my own son as ransom how will I not give you your own son.*" The Lord then gave me three more powerful scriptures as the words, now making four. That was the end to that battle. I stood up and told my wife. As far as I was concerned, it was done. The following month she was pregnant. Nine months later we had a boy, according to the spoken word I heard in my ear of the spirit. It could come while reading the Bible as if a portion is just lifted into your spirit. It could come while listening to the message and it could come while meditating, praying, or even doing something else entirely. Rhema is the spirit-enhanced arrow of the word shot at your spirit to produce faith for the now. The faith produced this way is what you start shooting through your mouth in confession against the mountain and inheritance will most surely manifest. I told my wife immediately to print out those scriptures and paste them in all possible places at home and in her office so she could see and confess them day and night. The devil of miscarriage could not withstand the arrow of the spirit, so they ran and we had the manifestation of our inheritance of fruitfulness and replenishing the earth.

The spoken word shouldn't just come to you once in a while or when you are in trouble. It should be your dwelling place and daily living. Joshua was told that once he was given to studying, brooding upon, and muttering the word (logos) day and night, he would be shown what it would take (rhema) to succeed every time, **Joshua 1:8.** To succeed here means to make profit out of life and Jesus said profitability is down to the spoken word or rhema not the written letter or the logos, **John 6:63.**

Anyone can read the Bible once you are educated, but the profit of inheritance spoken about in any passage only comes when the word comes into your spirit. When the word comes into your spirit, your duty is to keep saying it, make it your present reality. God said it when it was written as logos for you to study. Now he is saying it again to your spirit as rhema just as David said once has God spoken twice have I heard it. Once you hear what God has said, you should start saying it, too.

Let your conduct be without covetousness; be content with such things as you have. For He Himself has said, I will never leave you nor forsake you. So we may boldly say: The LORD is my helper; I will not fear. What can man do to me...Hebrews 13:5-6.

The Bible doesn't say because God has said it then whatever will be will be. For what he has said to be, we are to make it so by boldly declaring what he said. When you keep saying you have what the word says you have, even when you can't see it, you will soon have what the word says you have. When you keep saying you are what the word says you are, even when you don't feel like it, you will soon be what the word says you are. The word of God is given to you in order to help you take your eyes away from what is not yours and focus you on what is yours so you can have it. The word of God is given to help you see and focus on who you are so you can become just that, regardless of what others say you are.

Chapter 8

It's Your Faith For Your Inheritance

In the school of faith, inheritance is a place rather than a thing, a place of power, wisdom, riches, wisdom, strength, glory, and honor. When God took the Israelites out of Egypt, it was more than a geographical relocation as far as God was concerned. It was relocation into a place of inheritance. God called that land a land that flowed with milk and honey, but literally no milk or honey flowed on the street. There is more to the land in the school of inheritance than meets the eye. It has nothing to do with the fertility of the land because in that same land God said he would send drought and famine with scarcity of food if the people turned away from his ways. God did not give them money when they got in, but he gave them a place of riches as inheritance, a place of wisdom so much that he said the other nations would see the wisdom in manifestations in the kind of results they would be pulling against all odds. God would rather take you to the place of riches than to give you money. Money is just one of the inhabitants in the land of riches, and once you inherit the land, money has no choice than to obey and answer to whatever you do with your hand. Experiences have shown me that travelling abroad is not equal to getting into your land of inheritance. Many strugglers, beaten and battered destinies are in every land. Nevertheless, the land of inheritance is a place of arrival no matter where you are now and how bad the situation is now. You can fix your gaze on the place you are aiming at, regardless of present pain and insults.

By faith Abraham obeyed when he was called to go out to the place which he would receive as an inheritance. And he went out, not knowing where he was going...Hebrews 11:8

Once faith steps into a promise, it there and then becomes an inheritance. It stays in the family even while it is yet to manifest physically. For an adult to embark on a journey not knowing where he was going is embarrassing enough, but faith that lay hold of inheritance cannot wait until all things are equal or for an enabling and conducive environment.

We saw the written word of God coming to us as the logos or the idea and mindset of God concerning us. The written word is meant to give you hope or, in other words, set a destination in front of you to keep gazing at.

For whatever things were written before were written for our learning, that we through the patience and comfort of the Scriptures might have hope... Romans 15:4.

Hope here means a foreseeable future in your finances, career, family, health, and the entirety of your life. The kind of immediate and latter future you should be gunning for is what has been written down as the logos or idea of God concerning you. Nothing should paint another picture in your mind's screen apart from this written word. This painted picture is called hope. But hope can never deliver the goods. It can only show you what the goods are. To make the inheritance a present reality, you need to keep interacting with the word of God, which paints the hope until it brings faith to you.

When the specific word of God comes to you, the result will be faith, even the faith that says and does. Once faith came to Abraham, he obeyed, moving in the direction of his hope. Hope as an anchor for the soul, which is the home of emotion, will always elicit good feelings and happiness with invigoration, but the goods will only be delivered by faith. You can have hope of prospering from now until Jesus comes and be raptured a poor man or woman. To make the riches a present reality, you need faith to draw the hope near you by speaking forth and doing what the same word said. Abraham obeyed by physically moving in the direction the word spoken to him pointed. It takes the obedience born out of faith to enter into inheritance. "Name it and claim it" will not do but as you are naming and claiming it, you need to also do it. There is always something to do in faith.

Faith Helps You to Stand on Your Lot

Therefore, having been justified by faith, we have peace with God through our Lord Jesus Christ, through whom also we have access by faith into this grace in which we stand, and rejoice in hope of the glory of God...Romans 5:1-2.

Whatever comes from heaven is only accessible on earth through faith. It takes faith to create an inroad in your mind into what God has made available for you in Christ Jesus. The children of Israel did and had everything in the wilderness except faith, and God said they could not enter the land. The only ones granted access are the ones who had another sprit or another mindset born of faith. The place of inheritance in any area of your life is the place of rest where all struggles in that area end, but it takes a faith key for the door of access into such rest to be opened, **Hebrews 4:1-6.**

No matter how beautiful and marvelous the inheritance is, no matter how desperate you want it, the period of developing faith for it is a must. The reason is because just as it takes faith to access it, you will also need faith to keep it. The children of Israel desperately wanted to leave the wilderness, move into the Promised Land, and enjoy the milk and honey, thinking that the only obstacle of life was the hunger and the thirst they were facing. God rather would have them develop faith for living, which comes by an awareness (knowledge) of every word that proceeds out the Lord's mouth. God knew that entering the land was not the end of challenges. There were giants to displace and resist. There were wild beasts to destroy, and there was also a self in them to be put under, all of which takes greater faith.

It is easier to get married than to stay married, to be healed than to stay healthy, and to live on benefit than to be the one benefiting the needy. It is much easier to be pitied in defeat than to be celebrated and accepted in victory, getting it in life is not as tasking as to keeping it. This was seen in the prodigal son. To get an inheritance was the easiest thing for him, but to keep it was impossible. The bulk of what you are developing while God is working on you through his word and spirit to enter into what he had already given is the faith to keep it once you get it. No matter the level of the manifestation of the inheritance here on earth, it is nothing compared to what God has reserved for you in eternity. Whatever we partake of here is like a bucket from an ocean compared to what awaits us in heaven, knowing full well that whatever we receive here on earth is just a release from our heavenly inheritance stored beyond the clouds. In order not to miss the ultimate for the present manifestations, God allows you to develop faith along the way. It is this faith that keeps you in God no matter what you touch or taste as goodness or challenge here on earth.

Blessed be the God and Father of our Lord Jesus Christ, who according to His abundant mercy has begotten us again to a living hope through the resurrection of Jesus Christ from the dead, to an

inheritance incorruptible and undefiled and that does not fade away, reserved in heaven for you, who are kept by the power of God through faith for salvation ready to be revealed in the last time.1 Peter 1:3-5.

Faith for inheritance therefore is not just for collecting but also for keeping and preservation of the collector, you cannot walk with God into your inheritance and be lost on the way, even when you make mistakes on the way God will bring you back to the right path as a shepherd. God is not a wicked God. He is not baiting us with heaven and scaring us with hell. He built heaven's mansions for us and is determined we occupy them. It takes unbelief, doubt, and faithlessness to stop walking with God. This was why on most occasions when Jesus was talking of hell while on earth, he was addressing the unbelieving and self-righteous Pharisees or doubting scribes. I need to show you how to deal with faithlessness, unbelief, and doubt, which are three different cousins that stand against receiving and manifestation of that which God had given you, heaven included.

Evil Heart of Unbelief

Beware, brethren, lest there be in any of you an evil heart of unbelief in departing from the living God...Hebrews 3:12

Unbelief is a state of the heart that comes from the manipulations of devil, so it is called an evil heart. The heart of unbelief is hardened, cannot be appealed to or persuaded and this is sad. Have you not seen folks who say things like, "I know the Bible said so, but this other opinion is my own stand on the issue." These are people whose minds are almost made up on what Christianity ought to be even before they are born again, so nothing moves them again in the word. They have a readymade religious or cultural outlook and view of Christianity. They would rather argue than learn, no matter what God is doing in the midst of his people. Once it does not fit in into their "right doctrine," they are unpersuasive. When such are sick, no matter how many people God is healing around the world, they believe healing is not for today's church. The promises of God sound and look too good wherever there is unbelief, so they draw back or stagger away from it. What makes people stagger at the precious promises of God is unbelief. For someone in unbelief, there is always a good argument why the promises are not for them or anyone, for that matter. Maybe they saw someone who believed God in sickness and still died or someone who is fervent in church and still had a misfortune or someone who has "been believing" and has not seen a change or a man of God whose countenance they dislike. If Abraham was going to go by that, he would not have had Isaac. Twenty-five years is too long to wait for a child. Every time Abraham came home to tell his friend of his fresh encounter with God, all he had to show for it were promises upon promises and nothing more than promises, but he was never in unbelief.

And being not weak in faith, he considered not his own body now dead, when he was about an hundred years old, neither yet the deadness of Sarah's womb, he staggered not at the promise of God through unbelief, but was strong in faith, giving glory to God...Romans 4:19-20.

Don't get it wrong, unbelief is always built on something. There is always an excuse or example to give. The only thing is that unbelief considers all other parameters except what God has said. Whereas the only parameter of expectation for faith in you is the word of God and not any other experience that runs contrary to the word. The two languages of unbelief are shown below:

Can God?

The first question upon which unbelief is built is "can God do it." Can God use all these preachers nowadays to perform miracles, can God bless someone like me, can God solve this kind of great problem, can God do anything for this person. Kenneth E. Hagin of blessed memory said he discovered that some young non-bigoted but "not so strong" believers were receiving more healing and blessings than many well-established saints in one church he pastored long ago. The root cause was that the young believers and the other non-bigoted ones had simple faith to receive while the self-righteous "full grown" ones were there judging and questioning.

And they tested God in their heart by asking for the food of their fancy Yes, they spoke against God, they said, Can God prepare a table in the wilderness? Behold, he struck the rock, so that the waters gushed out, and the streams overflowed. Can He give bread also? Can He provide meat for His people? Therefore the LORD heard this and was furious, so a fire was kindled against Jacob, and anger also came up against Israel, because they did not believe in God, and did not trust in His salvation...Psalms 78:18-22.

No matter the move of God, unbelief makes people question his presence and his ability to deliver. Anything evil needs to be repented of or resisted in faith, same with the heart of unbelief. Once you have seen your inheritance in his word, no matter what the situation is right now, God can furnish a table for you in the present wilderness and give you water in the current desert. If your heart says contrary, repent of it and resist that devil by building your faith in God's word the more in that particular area of your life.

Does God Care?

The second question on which unbelief is built is "does God really care?" The pain of the challenges, the shame of enduring, and the seemingly unending dark horizon can make the heart to ask such a question. If your conclusion about God is based on what you feel, see, or hear rather than on what is written of him, faith will always be shaky. The moment your heart starts thinking God does not care, repent and resist. It is your adversary trying to manipulate your heart toward unbelief.

And when Pharaoh drew near, the children of Israel lifted their eyes, and behold, the Egyptians marched after them. So they were very afraid, and the children of Israel cried out to the Lord. Then they said to Moses, because there were no graves in Egypt, have you taken us away to die in the wilderness? Why have you so dealt with us, to bring us up out of Egypt? Is this not the word that we told you in Egypt, saying, let us alone that we may serve the Egyptians'? For it would have been better for us to serve the Egyptians than that we should die in the wilderness... Exodus 14:10-12.

Nobody would be happy caught between the Red Sea and a pursuing vicious Pharaoh. The experience of life at times can be hurtful but unbelief will only complicate the problem. In fact, unbelief would rather you stay in bondage quietly with no challenge than to enter an everlasting breakthrough and reach rest of inheritance through a light affliction. When the light affliction as it was for Paul comes, because you are not feeling God does not mean he cares less. God and feelings are not one and same. Even when there is stress, clear your mind of unbelief that suggests God does not care. Stop the thought, strengthen your word, stand, and avoid backsliding.

Unstable Mind of Doubt

Doubt denies people from having what has already been received in faith. For example, when you pray the word of God on an issue and obtain the "yes it is done" in your spirit, the substance of confidence is likely the only thing you will have to hold on to while waiting in faith for the manifestation of what had been received in prayer.

But let him ask in faith, with no doubting, for he who doubts is like a wave of the sea driven and tossed by the wind. For let not that man suppose that he will receive anything from the Lord, he is a double-minded man, unstable in all his ways... James 1:6-7.

Doubt means a double mind. One says, yes, it is done, the other says, no, it is not yet done. It is a reflection of the instability of the inner man. The outer man reacts according to a signal picked up by the senses or mental intuition while the inner man is a Spirit, a man of faith whose reaction is based on the light within. The dominant entity eventually takes the upper hand whenever you are dealing with any issue of life. Peter's inner man initiated the walking on water at the word of Jesus, but the dominant part of him as of then soon subdued the supernatural once he saw by his senses the boisterous wind.

And immediately Jesus stretched out His hand and caught him, and said to him, "O you of little faith, why did you doubt... Matthew 14:31

The man of faith in him was too little, just like a big lorry with a little engine, not much could be done. Thomas had to see and touch to believe and Jesus said he was a doubter because his faith was built on senses, thereby acting on mental accent rather than the inner man's conviction. Doubt is a reflection of the flesh dominating the spirit, a weak inner man that makes people remain fearful on an issue even though they've just finished praying or fasting. The truth is that you can't build your inner man in the place of asking while asking. You only use the one you have built earlier on. Praying in the Holy Ghost is the sure way of building your inner man up as an edifice that cannot be dominated by your senses or flesh.

But you, beloved, build yourselves up [founded] on your most holy faith [make progress, rise like an edifice higher and higher], praying in the Holy Spirit...Jude 20

Remember James said the doubtful man has more than one mind. The unification of the many minds takes place in the place of praying in the spirit. Note above that the word said "an" edifice will then evolve. Just one singular edifice can walk on water, slay giants, quench a fiery furnace, and receive what has been given, no matter what the senses say. An edifice of inner man well built in prayer will suspend the fear of losing with the faith of having.

Art of Faithlessness

To be faithless does not mean you don't have faith but lack it when needed. You own it but it is absent when needed, and it can't be brought to the scene. Unlike unbelief, your heart is not evil to limit God's ability or question his good intention neither are your senses dominating you to doubt but rather you see your faith as insignificant or incapable of addressing the issue at hand, so you abandon it all together. It is like owning a car and owning the key but when it is time to drive it, you find you've left the key in the house because you thought it is not significant and so you get stranded.

Now it happened, on a certain day that He got into a boat with His disciples. And He said to them; Let us cross over to the other side of the lake. And they launched out. But as they sailed He fell asleep. And a windstorm came down on the lake, and they were filling with water, and were in jeopardy. And they came to Him and awoke Him, saying, Master, Master, we are perishing!

Then He arose and rebuked the wind and the raging of the water. And they ceased, and there was calm. But He said to them, where is your faith? And they were afraid, and marveled, saying to one another, who can this be? For He commands even the winds and water, and they obey Him...Luke 8:22-25

When you hear God's word, faith comes to you. When you act on God's word, faith is made available on the scene. Your action is what validates the availability of faith, not your exclamation or crying at the challenge. The true value of faith is in its availability by corresponding action. The word says that the work done by faith is the only proof that the faith is available, **James 2:14-26.**

And in Lystra a certain man without strength in his feet was sitting, a cripple from his mother's womb, who had never walked, this man heard Paul speaking. Paul, observing him intently and seeing that he had faith to be healed, said with a loud voice, Stand up straight on your feet and he leaped and walked...Act 14:8-10.

What did Paul see as faith in the man? It must have been some actions, and maybe the man was shouting "I can't remain the same" and probably trying to stand on weak legs. He was not sitting down nodding and doing nothing. Paul saw faith in the man by the man's action.

Faith for inheritance is an acting faith, a doing faith, faith that is persuaded of divine ability to bring into manifestation what has been promised and given through Christ. Faith for inheritance is void of doubt. It will wait until God's word is given. The same word becomes flesh by producing results in whichever area of life he is dealing with. Faith for inheritance does not settle for an alternative, will not take a river instead of an Ocean, will want the best God can offer, and want to be the best he can become in God.

Chapter 9

Patient Unto Inheritance

Patience does not wait for things to happen or to be done, patience waits for what had happened and has been done even though it is not yet seen. Patience waits for the manifestation of what had already been made to happen and obtained through faith. **Mark 11:24.** Having all you are called to have and being all you are called to be is a journey of patience, a race like marathon, a life time race that requires a level of endurance. The manifestation and unfolding of your inheritance is a lifetime journey that culminates in eternal rest with the groom one day. This is the reason why it is not proper for Christians to have a different race for finances, another one for health, and one for power with another for glory, running many races at the same time, seeking survival and prominence here and there as the heathen do. There is only one race that is set before each of us. Running it right requires patience. In it are all you need to have and all you have to become. It is the race of inheritance.

Wherefore seeing we also are compassed about with so great a cloud of witnesses, let us lay aside every weight, and the sin which doth so easily beset us, and let us run with patience the race that is set before us, looking unto Jesus the author and finisher of our faith; who for the joy that was set before him endured the cross, despising the shame, and is set down at the right hand of the throne of God...Hebrews 12:1-2 (KJV).

The same race of inheritance was what Christ ran to become the savior and have all he has today, including a name above all names, which he obtained as an inheritance for himself from the father. The same race set Christ on the right hand of the throne where he obtained the eternal inheritance we have been talking about for the saints. The principal factor in the success of the race is the patience or endurance, as other versions of the Bible put it. For clarity's sake, we shall stick to the word patience.

Listening to the testimony of how a situation turned better overnight for your neighbor, at times, can be discouraging to the extent that you will start asking questions and developing fear that maybe something is wrong with you. But nothing is wrong with you except destiny. Abraham would probably have suffered immensely at the hand of today's preacher almost to the point of losing hope and faith in the spoken word he heard from God years back when Isaac was not yet manifest. He would probably have been diagnosed with demonic possession or oppression that would require special deliverance from clueless specialists. In patience, Abraham was not idle and doing nothing. Patience is not folding your hands waiting for whatever will happen to happen.

Abraham, in patience, was busy strengthening his faith through divine persuasions, thereby giving glory to God for what had been given. Jesus said once faith receives something in prayer, staying in faith will make the receiver have that which has been received. The staying in faith for the manifestation of what faith has received is what is referred to as patience. When you have a revelation of the word on a particular area of your inheritance, faith will come to you. As you keep confessing and working that which you now believe, you need patience for the manifestation to come. You will not start seeing money the day you come to the awareness and start walking in the faith of your inheritance of riches in God. It will take patience for physical wealth to be built and thus enjoyed. The national lottery cannot give a Christian his inheritance. Someone cannot dash you your inheritance, but you will need to work it out. Run it out as a race with patience.

My brethren, count it all joy when you fall into various trials, knowing that the testing of your faith produces patience. But let patience have its perfect work, that you may be perfect and complete, lacking nothing... James 1:2-4.

Patience is said to be a product of tried faith, rather than just an action. Patience is a state of being that produces a kind of action or doing. When you believe God for it, the resistance and seeming lack of manifestation of what you have obtained in faith is what God allows to produce patience as a character in you. What do I need character for, you will say, seeing all I need is my inheritance. The truth is that we don't think we need what we need most times until the need arises. The wisdom in the wise virgins was in their knowing what they needed beyond the immediate and stocking up now therefore.

Real Life Lessons

The reason why life seems like a wicked stage play and frustrating unfolding scenes of challenges at times is because *there is no rehearsal to life before you act it out for real.* If Adam had rehearsed the fall, there would not have been one when the real stage was set. If Judas Iscariot had rehearsed the betrayal of Jesus Christ and the unfolding events that followed, the story would have changed. *The reason we are dismayed and feel frustrated as we act out life is simply because most of the scenes take us by surprise.* The despair and helplessness felt when suddenly the doctor diagnoses a growth in the body is essentially due to the element of surprise in the appearance of the sickness from "nowhere" and the uncertainty of where it will lead. If you rehearsed it before and were healed, and came out healthier, stronger, and more fulfilled in life, you probably would be the one applying for it, seeing the outcome is fantastic. The cruel reality is that there is no room for rehearsal in the unfolding scenes of life. Most of what we see as challenges would have been praised as elevator if we have rehearsed them, made and corrected the mistakes, perfected the routine, and saw the outcome as very pleasant.

Beware that you do not forget the LORD your God by not keeping His commandments, His judgments, and His statutes which I command you today, lest when you have eaten and are full, and have built beautiful houses and dwell in them; and when your herds and your flocks multiply, and your silver and your gold are multiplied, and all that you have is multiplied; when your heart is lifted up, and you forget the LORD your God who brought you out of the land of Egypt, from the house of bondage; who led you through that great and terrible wilderness, in which were fiery serpents and scorpions and thirsty land where there was no water; who brought water for you out of the flinty rock; who fed you in the wilderness with manna, which your fathers did not know, that He might humble you and that He might test you, to <u>do you good in the end.</u> Deuteronomy 8:11-16.

The sweetness of victory is always at the end of any race, not in the middle or beginning. The celebration, taking of medals, waving a flag, and recognition as a champion and world record holder do not happen in the middle of the race no matter how fast you are at that point. God said the ultimate good was reserved for the latter end of their race in the wilderness, the ultimate good of having it the way you want it. But what was the need for waiting when everything seemed slow and stagnant, when they had to go through a place described as "terrible" by God himself and face fiery things and acute needs? Was it a punishment for their sin? Of course not. The change from 40 days of waiting to 40 years was as a result of their sin, but enduring the hardship for just 40 days as originally planned was not.

Challenges are always meant to last for a while. Paul called it light affliction, which is but for a moment. It is never meant as punishment but as an avenue to learn the real lesson of life, which will be needful in the high and lofty place which you are going. The land they were going was marked out as a land of plenty to eat and drink. No wonder the main challenges they had on the way involved food and drink. When you are going into your inheritance in a particular area, it is not uncommon that the area is where you will face the greatest challenges. Most pastors with large congregations always tell the story of struggling with growth at the onset even though they knew they were doing everything for growth in ministry. The scarcity of resources now should therefore point you to the fact that wealth is reserved ahead for you. The weakness of now should make you see the might in your inheritance. The heritage of power in the apostolic Church was unleashed after they were humiliated and made to feel ordinary by the power that be in their days, **Acts 4:1-31.**

To be perfect (mature), complete in understanding, entire, and wanting nothing even in the absence of material things, you need to have gone through the school of patience where the life of God in you becomes the real asset you are holding on to whether you are rich in the outside or poor, popular or unknown. The principal things that distinguish children from adult are the lessons of life they have picked up along the way rather than the size of their body. There are huge kids but they are still kids, and small adults but the difference is in their awareness or knowledge of life through the patience of learning. Kids throw tantrums at every slight provocation. They cry when they need something and they will disturb and disorganize the whole house. They will stop doing whatever they are doing right there and then. Adults can be hungry and still keep going while holding food in perspective. Adults don't weep because they don't have the latest garment even though they desire it. They don't retire from their jobs and lock themselves in because they couldn't get the latest car. The reason adults don't do these is because they have learned to hold life in perspective. This was the only reason God said the people went through the experience of wilderness that they may be able to hold life and material things (bread) in the right perspective based on the spoken word of God.

So He humbled you, allowed you to hunger, and fed you with manna which you did not know nor did your fathers know, that He might make you know that man shall not live by bread alone; but

man lives by every word that proceeds from the mouth of the LORD. Deuteronomy 8:3.

The reason they did not arrive in Canaan the day they left Egypt through faith was to learn this vital lesson in patience. God who miraculously parted the Red Sea and rained down bread had the capacity to transport them to Egypt that same day. God said if he had done so, they would not have learned the vital lesson in patience and would be ensnared by success in the land flowing with milk and honey. You need patience in the faith in order to learn the real lesson of life.

Possess Your Soul

The greatest asset you have on earth is your soul. Jesus said if a man trades on Wall Street to gain everything and earns material gains but loses his soul, he has not profited at all.

For what profit is it to a man if he gains the whole world, and loses his own soul? Or what will a man give in exchange for his soul. Mathew 16:26.

God's gifts are said to be good and perfect, not ensnaring and destructive. Whatever God will have you become and have you possess, he will want you to have it and still possess your precious soul. Jesus said it is possible to possess things and become something at the expense of one's soul. In fact, he called it an exchange, which indicates the material things were gained by barter. Suppose one gets it and builds a Church for God or pays tithe and contributes to other charities. Can the damage be undone? Not at all. It is better to be poor and possess your soul than to be rich and go to hell. It is better to be unknown, weak, and powerless and possess your soul than to have it all in exchange for your most prized possession. Are you saying once one gain these things he will automatically lose his soul? Not at all, a million times no. Jesus obtained all of them for us and still saved our souls so we could possess it.

How do I then possess inheritance or possessions in the face of challenges and needs and still come out with my soul intact?

And you will be hated by all for my name's sake. But not a hair of your head shall be lost. By your patience possess your souls. Luke 21:17-19.

The instinct of survival is what bring compromises of trade by barter in the face of needs and challenges, wanting it and wanting it bad and by all means no matter what it takes, even if it costs your soul. I grew up in a society where people join cults to get money, prominence, influence, and protection. Some even join to protect their posterity. But these cults are Satan worship, and the members' souls are given over to the devil in exchange for the material possessions. Many don't go this far in other parts of the world, but they still plunge their souls into many hurtful pits, trying to gain wealth, for lack of patience.

Mature Into Sonship

One of the major differences between the first and the last Adam is patience. The last Adam, Jesus Christ, learned obedience in patience through the things he suffered and became the author of eternal salvation to all that believed

Though He was a Son, yet He learned obedience by the things which He suffered. And having been perfected, He became the author of eternal salvation to all who obey Him. Hebrews 5:8-9.

In the book of James, we saw that patience produces perfection. Here we can see that what Christ was said to have suffered were the trials of his faith as a man, which produced patience that perfected him as a man, even though he was born perfect as God. Inheritance is kept under the elemental tutors until the possessor is matured through growth, which comes by patience. Moses was called of God to be a deliverer and he knew, but in haste he went and in haste he ran away also. What he needed just 10 more years to wait for came 30 years late and thus extended the sojourning of God's people from 400 years God told Abraham to 430 years. In God's school of inheritance, you cannot escape any lesson meant for you. All you can do is to extend the number of years it will take you to learn it, just like repeating a class.

Many destinies are tied to your own as it was for Moses. Your entering into the full possession of your purchased inheritance will emancipate many destinies, meet many needs and liberate many souls from the bondage of corruption the whole creation is subject to in hope. Doomed is humanity if the saviors in Zion are trapped in rat race of impatience, if the captains are locked up and the labor to birth the champions suffers unending delays.

The reality is, once patience is lacking, delay is inevitable. In the kingdom, impatience ultimately leads to delay, derailment and eventual denial. When I finished medical school, I suffered from Moses' syndrome and was impatient to see the outward manifestation of the treasures within. The resulting fall was so great that it took a decade for me to recover. I rushed out of the ministry I rushed into and vowed not to touch it with a long pole again. It took every grace and mercy in eternity for me to get my footing back almost 10 years later. All the growth and labor of love of the years behind, especially while I was in the University, seemed lost to impatience. All the grace and virtue of Christian living faded away quick. I was miserable, though making money. The journey I could not delay for probably two or three years got suspended and postponed for 10 years, only to start from the onset again!

Friend, you need patience to make your faith for inheritance of great value. The true test of believing is patience. When gold is tried in fire and what remains is gold, we know we had real gold. If what we get is ashes then what we had might have looked like gold but it was not gold. When faith like gold is tried, what comes out is patience. The trial of your faith works patience. If not, it is not faith that brings in the inheritance.

The Wisdom of Patience

Nobody loves to be delayed in life, but not all delay is evil. The difference between delay and patience is that with patience, there is growth in wisdom and advancement in spiritual stature even when not much physical change can be seen. Patience is wisdom, and patience brings wisdom. No matter how much a child is loved and cared for they are not given control of many things until a certain age simply because they lack the knowhow of managing such without self-destruction.

> ***Now I say that the heir, as long as he is a child, does not differ at all from a slave, though he is master of all, but is under guardians and stewards until the time appointed by the father...Galatians 4:1-2.***

Notice that the word "time" is the key word that unlocks the door of the said inheritance. The child's paternity is not in question, neither is the love of the father nor the availability of the bestowed inheritance. Notice also that while the child was being treated and tutored as a slave, he was still called the master of all meaning that what you have or what you are is not as important as who you are right now. The new creation is the master and heir of all the inheritance of God's kingdom, even though you don't look or feel like it right now. The patience of waiting until the appointed time can never be short circuited through prayer or fasting. A special offering would not do, neither will laying on of hands. No matter how well you feed a child to grow fast, there is a threshold beyond which it becomes malignant and abnormal. Can you imagine a 6 year old fully grown, a graduate of university, married with kids and controlling a vast conglomerate left by his father. Such would be called the freak of nature. No matter how much and how soon the father wants him to have all of the above a growing process tied to time is a must.

There are kids who look like adults until a demand is laid on their wisdom, and you will see that even though they have grown in stature same cannot be said of wisdom. There is a wisdom that comes with experience. Such wisdom was what killed Goliath when David came on the scene. Such wisdom was what God wanted the Israelites to learn in the wilderness for 40 days so they could put bread and life in the right perspective against the days of plenty. There is a part of wisdom you will learn through knowledge. There is a part that will come as impartation of the Holy Spirit, but there is also a vital part that will come through experience born over time in patience. None of these is a replacement for the other. No matter how much you know or how anointed you are, no one will put their life in your hands as passengers on an air plane when you don't have the requisite flying experience for pilot certification.

This is the litmus test to know if you are in patience or delay-*are you growing in it, are you learning new things that make for where you are going, is the giant in you evolving with higher strength and wisdom?* Once the answer is positive, you are on a ride of patience toward inheritance. We know that Abraham was in patience and not delay because, his persuasion had been worked upon in the waiting period so much that at the end of the day he was "fully" persuaded that whatsoever God said God was going to do; God was able to do it. **Romans 4:21**. If Abraham's persuasion was full at the onset, the Bible would not need to say that he was fully persuaded. Looking at some of Abraham's utterances to God and actions in earlier chapters of his journey of destiny, the same cannot be said of his persuasion even though he was in faith. It took patience to get there and eventually he had Isaac.

The wisdom Abraham got out of the experience of patience he had while waiting for Isaac was all he needed when called upon by God to offer Isaac for promotion in blessedness. He was persuaded God was able to raise the lad from the dead after killing him seeing he got him from his dead seed and the dead womb of Sarah from the onset. God marked Abraham's paper right and said. *"I have not started blessing you yet, now in blessing I will bless you."* **Genesis 22:1-19; Hebrews 11:17-19.**

The rope of destiny is learnt in patience. Mistakes are made, weaknesses are discovered, and the requisite strength developed. I was eager to be a doctor as a young man and headed for the university but one thing I noticed in the medical faculty is that they don't rush, neither are they in a hurry to graduate you. We saw the training as unnecessarily tough and long, but it paid off at last when liability of error in practice started looking us in the face as young practitioners. We also had the school shut down many times due to student unrest or lecturers' strikes, which were very many in my days. Whenever this happened and we were in the middle or even almost the end of the 12-week rotation in a clinical unit, we would be made to start that particular unit rotation all over again whenever the school resumed. It seemed unreasonable to us aspiring student who wanted to be doctors on time, but to the faculty it was a necessary delay to make temperate doctors with the right values that go with the profession out of us. There is a temperament and some values that go with your inheritance to prevent you making an accident of destiny after you may have gotten what you are meant to get and becoming what you are meant to become. Such temperaments and values are imbibed in the school of patience. Be therefore patient unto the possession of your purchased inheritance.

Yinka Akintunde

Chapter 10

The War Of Inheritance

Whichever way you look at it, the land that flows with milk and honey is also the land full of the giants. The reason why most people want luck rather than their inheritance is because luck is that which comes to you while you are just standing there doing nothing. The land of inheritance does not come by luck. It comes by war, and it takes fighting for it with all you have got to get it. What comes on a platter of gold in life is failure. Failure is the easiest thing to get in an exam. Just don't prepare, get in the hall and sleep, wake up, and submit an empty paper with your name and number and that is all. To take off in life requires a deliberate fighting of the inertia, a dissipation of energy against the holding force. The war of inheritance is not a coincidence or a happenstance. It is a contest well-orchestrated by the divine to make the final and a lasting champion out of you.

And the LORD God said to the woman, what is this you have done? The woman said, "The serpent deceived me, and I ate." So the LORD God said to the serpent: because you have done this, you are cursed more than all cattle, and more than every beast of the field; on your belly you shall go, and you shall eat dust all the days of your life. And I will put enmity between you and the woman, and between your seed and her Seed; He shall bruise your head, and you shall bruise His heel, Genesis 3:13-15.

The above conversation took place shortly after the devil deceived man out of his inheritance, and I would like you to see the wisdom of God in the judgment, because even in his judgment is love and wisdom for us.

The deception of man was made possible in the first place because of the friendship atmosphere that existed between him and the serpent. The conversation that led the thief of inheritance in was a smooth, friendly one that bordered on negotiation and agreement but the result was daylight robbery and stripping of glory and dignity. God said to forestall a repeat episode, a line of enmity has to be drawn between the man billed for inheritance and the thief of inheritance.

You need to know that on almost all occasions, the thief seems to strike first but his defeat is always final and eternal. Therefore when you strike in response, the battle is over. He is to bruise the feet while you crush the head. No matter how deadly the enemy strike is, it cannot go beyond mere bruising. Challenges and giants in the land that flows with milk and honey are therefore not capable or allowed to destroy you. They are mere feet bruising. What you are going through on the journey of destiny can be rough. They are only meant to alert your awareness to the reality of your enmity with the prince of this world and be conscious there is a war going on over your inheritance. The challenge is to provoke the greater one that lies dormant in you because you are not engaging him. It is so easy for a saint to live a normal, natural self-dependent life once the road is smooth and plain. It is easy to rely on the job for wealth and the earthly structures for existence and sustenance. It takes the rough in the going showing up for many of us to realize that in him alone we live and move and have our inheritance.

War Against self

The greatest war to fight in you becoming what you are called to be and having all you are called to have, is the war against your own self.

Now this I say, brethren, that flesh and blood cannot inherit the kingdom of God; nor does corruption inherit incorruption... 1 Corinthians 15:50.

The real you was born in Christ as spirit through new birth, but there is also a part of you born in human flesh, trained in the ways and manner of this world until you met Christ. No matter how nice, innocent, and kind your fleshly entity is, it cannot deliver the good. Before you were saved, you developed a personality based on your genes and environment. This personality was raised according to the will of your parents, teachers, family, friends, foes, and even society. Because of your various experience in life, you have grown to love or hate this personality. You do everything to nurture and protect it. You don't want this personality to lose out in the scheme of things, so you act in fear at times. Truth be said, the natural human personality is selfish. When God shows up in your life to lead you into your inheritance, the obvious reaction often is a stern resistance, especially if the terrain looks unfamiliar, feels rough, or not so promising for the foreseeable horizon.

You are familiar with a man called Lot in the Bible. Although he was not the one who rescued himself from the inferno of Sodom, he was self- protecting enough to tell his rescuer where he would rather settle in and inherit against divine suggestion. Genesis 19:17-22. He got a small plain out of self-preservation and ended up in a cave of ignominy and shame instead of the mountain of prominence and dignity.

Even though you didn't save yourself into the kingdom, there is always the tendency to want to apportion unto yourself the lots of the kingdom and if that which you want badly does not fall to you by divine appointment. There is always the tendency to grab it anyway no matter who is hurt. The fear of losing out is the greatest fear that has bred the most selfish species among humans. This is why Christ said if you love yourself too much at the expense of what God wants for you, you will lose out.

Then Jesus said to His disciples, "If anyone desires to come after me, let him deny himself, and take up his cross, and follow me, for whoever desires to save his life will lose it, but whoever loses his life for my sake will find it...Matthew 16:24-25.

Reading the build up to these profound statements in the preceding verses, you will notice that the man in question was given the exact kind of call given to those who eventually became the apostles of Jesus, but he blew it to self.

Self is a tool in the hand of Satan. Self has to be conquered for the devil's defeat on the cross to be obvious in your life. Many wrong marriages have been contracted by self even when God used all indications and circumstances to show that it won't work and must not be contracted. Many businesses have been started by self; many ministries are built on self – (*self-preservation as was in Adam and Eve*). They were convinced that God did not do enough to protect their interest. They could be better than God intended, the devil said. Many wonderful relationships planted on your way by God to enhance your journey of inheritance will only serve their purpose when you win over self. Do you know fasting is not a show of strength of how spiritual we are but a reminder and a form of exercise to remind you that the focus and attention cannot always be on your fleshly self? Have you not been in services where saints are said to be praising God and all the song is about them and their blessings and their cars and their enemies, everything about them except God and yet it is praise and worship to God!

Flesh and blood represent the carnal man. It cannot help in the journey of inheritance, and it does not inherit the kingdom of God. We live in a twisted world where you hear things like "*I will do it if it makes me happy.*" Well, God is not against your happiness. He is not a sadist in any way, but transient gratifications and corruptible happiness is not his perfect plan for you either. We have heard of people who die of complications from narcotics consumption, but they were happy while taking it, until the agony of premature death knocks on their door. Eve saw the happiness of eating the fruit before plucking it, but what she didn't see was the stripping and evacuation that would follow.

War against The Past

In having all you are meant to have and being all you are meant to be, one of the greatest wars you will fight is the war against your past, good or bad. The bad past is always the enemy of the good future while the good past is the enemy against the better future, both have to be conquered.

Brethren, I do not count myself to have apprehended; but one thing I do, forgetting those things which are behind and reaching forward to those things which are ahead... Philippians 3:13

Here was a man who had a measure of success but would not let past achievements stop him from his high call; such was the spirit of excellence spoken of Daniel and his three mates. Remember that the whole Israel was in captivity, which was not a pleasant experience, but here were Hebrew eunuchs or special palace assistants, a few who had found favor by God as prophesied and thus not suffering like others in captivity. There were many of them in Nebuchadnezzar's kingdom, but these four distinguished themselves by not relenting on the relative success they had but pressing further into their possibilities in God. When they were introduced in the book of Daniel, they were not lamenting and complaining about home. They were improving themselves for the task ahead, thus they were promoted to governors. The same principles got them promoted again until they were the best among many, the governors of the governors.

We don't always pay attention to how the past played a major role in the Israelites missing the land that was flowing with milk and honey. We need to know that these were a people oppressed for a significant part of 430 years by the people they grew up to know as neighbors and co-habitants of the land of Egypt. They have grown up to read meaning to other people's action, they have grown up to be suspicious and fend for their own interest. The case was made worse when Moses, whose past they knew, was now the one to lead them to a Promised Land. This was the same Moses who enjoyed what they didn't enjoy as far as they were concerned and the same Moses who killed someone and moved on the following day as if nothing happened yesterday. These people had neither seen nor heard God. It was therefore easy for them to be suspicious of God himself, especially a God who had Moses as his spokesman. When hunger and thirst showed up, all they could see was death. When they spied the land, all they could see was another giant who would become their task masters or even a worse one compared to the ones they left in Egypt, so they started campaigning for a return.

Moses himself had tried the rescue mission before and failed, so it was easy for him to point God to what he saw as his personal failing. Kindly send someone else, he said when called upon this time around. In all of these it was either the bad or the good past at work, but no past is good or bad enough to trade your better future for. Fight it now and move ahead.

Fight Now and Make Today Count

And Jabez called on the God of Israel saying, "Oh that you would bless me indeed, and enlarge my territory, that your hand would be with me, and that you would keep me from evil, that I may not cause pain!" So God granted him what he requested... 1 Chronicles 4:10.

Here was a man suffering a present pain because of a bad past. What he did was to make his warfare a present reality. Instead of weeping about yesterday, he fought today and won forever. Jesus had similar challenge when he began to teach, preach, and heal. The people who saw him grew up as a natural man started despising and questioning his supernatural claims and acts. When he began his ministry, he started doing and saying certain things that were not compatible with what they had known him to be. He started saying: *"am the bread of life," "come to me all that labor," "will you love to be made whole by me."* None of these were words or works of a carpenter, mind you, so they started reminding him of his past in case he forgot, lest he became delusional of whom he was in their view.

And when the Sabbath day was come, he began to teach in the synagogue: and many hearing him were astonished, saying, from whence hath this man these things? And what wisdom is this which is given unto him, that even such mighty works are wrought by his hands? Is not this the carpenter, the son of Mary, the brother of James, and Joses, and of Juda, and Simon? And are not his sisters here with us? And they were offended at him...Mark 6:2-3.

Christ did not stop doing what he was doing neither did he stop aiming for what he aimed for because of their offences. That was then, this is now, was his attitude to everyone reminding him of the past. Then he was the son of Mary but now he is the son of God in whom the father was well pleased and whom everyone must hear! You need to put your feet down now in spite of the past; if you will become who you are meant to be and have all you are meant to have.

Yesterday's failure needs today's womb to be nurtured and your present strength to be relevant in your destiny again, but you can abort it today and deny it every chance for survival so it doesn't ruin and stop your glorious possibilities. There is something called referred pain in medical science. This is a situation where pain in one part of the body is seeking expression and relevance in other part to complicate the torment of the bearer. Such is the way past pains, disadvantages, and failures want to operate. They seek relevance in your today and particularly in your future. It is your duty to refuse them admission in your luggage now.

Cut off anyone or any voice who wants to help you nurture such evil seeds and move on with your life in God. You don't need to be agreeable to people's opinion of you. You won't get it because people say you can get it. You will get it because God said you can get it. You won't be it because people said you can be it. You will be it because God said that is who and what you are. Eternal facts are surer than any laboratory evidence. Fight the present wiles and taunts of the enemy with the truth you see in God now. The present realities of the gospel are the antidote to past pains and challenges you have suffered.

<u>Fight for Your Future</u>

Be sober; be vigilant; because your adversary the devil walks about like a roaring lion, seeking whom he may devour.. 1 Peter 5:8

This is not a word for someone who has been devoured or someone who is being devoured. It is a word for someone whose future is a target of the wicked. The enemy is never scared of anyone's past because he survived it one way or the other. He might not mind your present seeing he is coping, but the enemy hates and is afraid of your future because it has not been seen nor heard, neither has it entered into the heart of anyone. The devil also has fear of the unknown and is scared of the element of surprise, so he plans to ruin the future before it happens. All of today's challenges are targeted at you so you can abandon your glorious tomorrow. Peter was made to deny Christ today as a disciple so that he could not be the apostle strengthening others tomorrow. We are so comfortable today at times that when God's spirit is constraining us against impending danger, we are not sensitive enough to pick the signal and so many walk into ditches.

Then Jacob was left alone; and a Man wrestled with him until the breaking of day. Now when He saw that He did not prevail against him, He touched the socket of his hip; and the socket of Jacob's hip was out of joint as He wrestled with him. And He said; let me go, for the day breaks. But he said I will not let you go unless you bless me. So He said to him, what is your name?

He said, Jacob. And He said your name shall no longer be called Jacob, but Israel; for you have struggled with God and with men, and have prevailed. Then Jacob asked, saying, Tell me your name, I pray. And He said why it that you ask about my name is? And He blessed him there...Genesis 32:24-29.

You will wonder what Jacob was fighting for. He had the birth right already. At this point, he was no more a struggling man trying to make the ends meet. He was rich in material wealth. He had a family of his own and was an entrepreneur working for himself now, yet he wrestled. Jacob had fought many battles in the past and won. In his words, he was not a young lad again seeing he crossed Jordan with his staff as a supporting rod, yet he wrestled. Ahead of Jacob lies Esau, a man who had an axe to grind with him. The truth of the matter is, it is better to prevail here before Esau came with vengeance.

Praying when things are already damaged for restoration is a wise job, but praying ahead for things to be preserved against damage is a wiser way. Being healed is great, but staying healthy is better. If the anointing that heals is properly discerned in time of health, the same anointing will ward off sickness from coming. God who heals was revealed primarily as one who will not allow the sickness to come in the first place. **Exodus 15:26.** God said instead of being sick tomorrow and waiting to be healed, work in my word today to stay healthy tomorrow. Instead of begging me to help you out of debt tomorrow, learn my financial wisdom and live it today, God is saying. The victories of tomorrow are a product of today's fighting. The wisdom of tomorrow is a product of today's knowledge. Invest in your future today. Don't leave the journey to the last minute. Work today while it is called day. Tomorrow comes when no man can work. It is never too late today. You can start now.

Who in the days of his flesh, when he had offered up prayers and supplications with strong crying and tears unto him that was able to save him from death, and was heard in that he feared...Hebrews 5:7.

Christ was shown here fighting death before he faced death. He actually beat death before he died, because the Bible said he was heard by him that was able to save him from the death after praying while he was still alive.

No wonder the same Christ was raised from the dead by the power of God through the Holy Spirit while in the grave. **Romans 1: 1-4.**

<u>Prevail at All Cost</u>

It is not enough to start your financial journey in God. It is better to end it there. It is not enough to start having all you will in God. It is better to have everything you will in him. It is not enough to start being what you want to be in God. It is better to be all you love to be in him. To prevail is to stay through, not to give up because of challenges and not to give in to attractive distractions.

Now the sons of Reuben the firstborn of Israel — he was indeed the firstborn, but because he defiled his father's bed, his birthright was given to the sons of Joseph, the son of Israel, so that the genealogy is not listed according to the birthright; yet Judah

prevailed over his brothers, and from him came a ruler, although the birthright was Joseph's...1 Chronicles 5:1-2.

Wonderful, is this not the way life plays out in general, that the most gifted and the most qualified necessarily don't become the most successful. The birthright was taken from Ruben and given to Joseph for obvious reason. In spite of that, Joseph's lineage could not produce the messiah, which was the sole reason for the birthright.

How did Judah bring his lineage in God to reckoning in inheritance? Simply by prevailing.

What did he prevail against? He prevailed against all we have been discussing above and every other challenge that came his way. You are not utterly disadvantaged until you quit the fighting and finally give up. The challenges of life are opportunities for you to bring yourself to reckoning. Remember that Christ himself got your inheritance for you by prevailing first. He got it not because he was a nice and gentle man or because he was the son of God. He got it because he prevailed.

And one of the elders said unto me, Weep not: behold, the Lion of the tribe of Judah, the Root of David, hath prevailed to open the book, and to lose the seven seals thereof...Revelation 5:5.

The worthiness of Christ to open the book, be a redeemer, and obtain inheritance for you was premised on his prevailing. As a young boy, I was made to believe that Christ and Satan were fighting in the grave or hell and then Christ won the fight and so the resurrection we celebrate is Easter. But the word has something contrary to say to that fight. Christ was not fighting the devil in the grave. All Christ needed to conquer the devil was his death and without lifting a finger further, he prevailed.

Even when Satan rebelled in heaven, God was not throwing fists and punches and carrying grenades to fight the devil. It was the company of angel that defeated Satan. We ascribe so much more power to the devil than he actually ever had! He rather conquered the one who had the power of death, even the devil, through death. Jesus conquered the devil by facing what the devil had in his hand as a threat to all humanity, the same weapon he was using to keep everyone in bondage. **Hebrews 2:14-15.**

People don't prevail by shying away from their challenges. They prevail by confronting the challenges all square until the tide turns in their favor. Jesus could have blamed Adam and Eve and serpent, but he didn't waste his energy on such mudslinging and cheap emotional blackmail. All he wanted was victory and victory he got. He went head long into the grave and came out head high far above death and grave. Big stuffs of the kingdom are not for wimps. People who don't want trouble, people who don't want to ruffle the world or religious feathers hardly amount to much in the journey of inheritance. One of my most referred mentors said, "It takes a lion heart to take a lion share." Nothing could be truer. Believers' inheritance is essentially of the spirit. Taking a warring stand against spirit entities contending for the goods is the first principle in taking your own land that flows with milk and honey.

CHAPTER 11

DIVINE ENABLING FOR INHERITANCE

When all is said and done, you need to realize finally that it takes God's help to take what God gives and be what he wants you to be in him. The energy and strength to become comes from God himself.

Now Jacob went out from Beersheba and went toward Haran. So he came to a certain place and stayed there all night, because the sun had set. And he took one of the stones of that place and put it at his head, and he lay down in that place to sleep. Then he dreamed, and behold, a ladder was set up on the earth, and its top reached to heaven; and there the angels of God were ascending and descending on it. And behold, the LORD stood above it and said: I am the LORD God of Abraham your father and the God of Isaac; the land on which you lie I will give to you and your descendants. Also your descendants shall be as the dust of the earth; you shall spread abroad to the west and the east, to the north and the south; and in you and in your seed all the families of the earth shall be blessed. Behold, I am with you and will keep you wherever you go, and will bring you back to this land; for I will not leave you until I have done what I have spoken to you...Genesis 28:10-15.

Here we saw Jacob, a man of inheritance, a man who shall have what God would have him had and become all that God would have him become, yet God said he God was the one holding him and who would do everything for him. No wonder Paul the Apostle said it is this same God who helps us to will and to do all of his good pleasure. It is God's good pleasure for you to have all he had given and to become all he had purposed for you as inheritance but you need God's enabling as was for Jacob to get there. The children of Israel were the ones who spied the land of Canaan. They were the ones who fought the battle and occupied the land, yet the word of God said they got not the land by their own self. What helped Jacob can be simply described in what we flippantly share at the end of most meetings today as the doxology. It was *the grace of the Lord, the Love of God, and the presence or the fellowship of his Holy Spirit* that was summarized in Jacob's encounter above. The divine enabling necessary for you to enter and lay hold of your divinely appointed inheritance is made available through this three-fold cord.

The grace of Our Lord, Jesus Christ

The first issue we need to settle here is the fact that whatever God ever gave to mankind was as a result of his own free will by grace and not our entitlement. In a closer sense, all Christian inheritance came by the grace of God made available to us through our Lord Jesus. There was no United Nations committee set up to press God for the inheritance. It was not a product of someone's good work but the out flowing of the grace of God through Christ Jesus. Salvation was a product of grace, for by grace you are saved through faith not of works. If salvation came by grace, every other thing that came through salvation can only be obtained when grace is in place as well. *It takes grace for grace to deliver; it takes grace to receive what grace has got to offer. Inheritance is a matter of grace for grace.*

And of his fullness have all we received, and grace for grace...John 1:16.

No wonder the word of inheritance was called the "word of his grace." I know we are used to seeing grace as an unmerited favor, but that can never do enough justice to the enormous subject of grace from the scripture's perspective. Grace is truly an unmerited favor, but grace is far more than unmerited favor.

<u>Grace is the strength for running</u>

Christianity is a call unto a race, a race you run to obtain your own inheritance. All you need to have and to be are entrenched in the race set before you. As you arrive at the different stages of the race, the inheritance is unfolded unto you as prize for running each phase well, until you finish the race eventually for the ultimate prize and rewards in eternity. The principal factor in the race of inheritance is the strength to finish and not your speed of running or how smooth the track is. It is a lifelong race that requires you to be temperate in all things, and it is a marathon that requires enormous strength to remain on track.

Wherefore seeing we also are compassed about with so great a cloud of witnesses, let us lay aside every weight, and the sin which doth so easily beset us, and let us run with patience the race that is set before us... Wherefore we receiving a kingdom which cannot be moved, let us have grace, whereby we may serve God acceptably with reverence and godly fear...Hebrews 12:1-28.

The whole chapter 12 of Hebrews talks of Christian inheritance in the light of a race. It highlights how fainting is possible if care is not taken. Having said all, we were told to "have grace" and the deal will be done. It is easier to be something else and have just anything than being what God wants you to be and what he wants you to have. The reality is that you have been in pursuit of other things and many things for that matter before you knew the Lord, especially things that everyone else around you was pursuing. It is easier to settle for what is available around you than to pursue what is obtainable in your eternal inheritance. It takes the strength of grace to go all the way. When what comes into your hand as a prize at a particular stage of the race looks insufficient to meet the need at hand. It takes strength to keep running for the higher prize ahead. This was one of the areas in which the children of Israel had a problem. The water was not enough now neither was the bread sweet enough and yet they were expected to be running toward the land that flows with milk and honey. Grace will help you to keep running towards the better, even when what you have at hand now does not even qualify to be called good.

Grace is the needed help for building

Christianity is a call to build as a laborer in the master's house. You are called to build your own life as house according to a particular pattern that God himself reveals to you. You are also called to be a part-builder in the body of Christ. What you are to build is unique and different from others. The same goes for how you are to build, and it takes grace to build right. It is the will of God that every part of your life is well built and you are the one he employs to undertake the task as no one can build for you even though many people will be sent your way as gifts in helping build correctly. As you keep building, the prize of inheritance keeps showing up in your life in stages. In God's kingdom, the house you don't build you can't inhabit. Things are never left to chance and happenstance but every great thing is a product of a deliberate and conscious building endeavor. The famed woman with the issue of blood was not healed by luck or chance but by purpose. Jesus did not die by accident. It was a deliberate death that he might have a better resurrection. In God's kingdom, you can't be rich by chance. You can't be strong by chance nor wise by chance. Blessing glory and honor are not left to chance. They are all products of deliberate building of your life that show up as inheritance in stages even as you are building your life to divine pattern. Everyone who ever built something tangible in God did so by grace. Noah obtained grace and he built the ark, **Genesis 6:8.** Paul said he was a successful builder by the reason of the grace given to him as a master builder. If the master builder needed grace, you need it much more.

For we are God's fellow workers; you are God's field, you are God's building. According to the grace of God which was given to me, as a wise master builder I have laid the foundation, and another builds on it. But let each one take heed how he builds on it...1 Corinthians 3:9-10.

For your life to count in God's kingdom, you need to build it by grace. This grace is not a feeling neither is it nebulous. Paul knew it was given him so it is a tangible force with visible impact. If grace is given, it then can be obtained as we are admonished to come boldly to God's throne of grace to "obtain" grace needed to help us in the time of need, **Hebrews 4:16.** A time of building is a time of need. You need the constant supply of the right materials from God to build your life, and you need his guidance to get the pattern right. All of these needs are the help you obtain as grace when you seek God. How much your life takes off from the ground is function of how much it is built up from the ground. High-rise buildings are not products of luck but of concerted efforts put together by someone.

For every house is built by someone, but He who built all things is God...Hebrews 3:4

Every house could be your career, finances, family, and ministry and so on, while you are building such in your inheritance, you will need the partnership of God in building well. The only way God gets involved is by the way of grace or divine enabling to build.

Grace is the power to become

But by the grace of God I am what I am, and His grace toward me was not in vain; but I labored more abundantly than they all, yet not I, but the grace of God which was with me...1 Corinthians 15:10.

We said in your inheritance is all you ought to become and nothing is too big or too good for you as a King's kid. God is not averse to his children aiming high and being the best. As a father that is what he really wants you to be. You will need to labor in your inheritance in order to be the best. Don't be deceived, there is no free meal in destiny. The only difference is that while laboring, the grace will be with you as oil and grease of help. It will grant you the needed ability, wisdom, encouragement, and empowerment. You can't be the best surgeon unless you go through the rigors of medical training, no matter how blessed and anointed you are. Great business and conglomerates don't fall from heaven as a blessing. They are products of great mental, physical, and spiritual labors. The essence of grace is for the labor not to be in vain. The oil that greases the engine of your labor so you don't perspire and wear out or give up is called grace. When challenges come, it is grace that won't let you give in and give up. When results are not yet commensurate to the effort you are putting in, it is grace that will make you stay through for your harvest. It is therefore incomprehensible and unacceptable for a believer to commit suicide for whatever reason.

"I was early taught to work well as play. My life has been one long happy holiday, full of work and full of play. I dropped the worry on the way and God was good to me everyday"

These are wonderful words from John D. Rockefeller, a successful man reputed to be one of the richest men of all time, the first American billionaire. He was an avowed and a committed Christian who was not ashamed to trace his success and stupendous wealth to divine blessing from God even when the cynics mocked his assertion of faith. All that he said and quoted above simply described the grace of God at work in his life. A life full of work and yet lived as if it was all play! This is simply entering into the rest that inheritance has got to offer. May you get in there.

A portion of a chapter in a book is not enough to talk about the grace with which we have to do, but I would love you to know that grace is not out of reach the way religion portrays it. Grace is always made available by God. If it were not so, God wouldn't ask you to come boldly to the throne and obtain it. The word of God is the capsule of grace. As you take it in you are receiving grace, so Paul commended the Ephesians' saints to the "word" of God's grace. Looking down, battered, and beaten is not what qualifies you for grace. Delving into God's word consistently in all ways and manners you can is what makes grace available. ***Act 20:32.***

When you believe and act on God's word by faith, what you are doing is standing in grace. No wonder Paul said grace is for laboring and not to be received in vain.

Therefore, having been justified by faith, we have peace with God through our Lord Jesus Christ, through whom also we have access by faith into this grace in which we stand, and rejoice in hope of the glory of God...Romans 5:1-2

Grace is accessible through faith and faith comes by hearing God's word, therefore the enabling of grace comes into your life as you fellowship with God before his throne in prayers and give yourself earnestly to his word which produces faith for your access. Grace for every issue of life is accessible by faith for that area of your life, and faith for every issue of life comes by word for that area of life. As you build yourself up in God's word grace comes to you, as you keep acting out your faith in that word grace keeps abounding towards you by Christ.

The Love of God

It was said to her, the older shall serve the younger as it is written, "Jacob I have loved", but Esau I have hated. What shall we say then? Is there unrighteousness with God? Certainly not...Romans 9:12-14.

We saw in the beginning of the chapter how God vowed to help Jacob become what he was meant to be and have what he was meant to have, but behind the whole encounter was the love of God. It is easy to teach all the principles of success and Christian ethics and doctrine and forget the love of God. You need to realize that the triumph of life is hinged on your understanding the love of God and living it. Even prayers are answered on the platform of divine love. In **Ephesians 3:13-22**, talking about saints not fainting in the face of adversity but inheriting the glory of triumph, talking of having your prayer answered over and above. Paul the Apostle only prayed that such saints should be given the revelation of the father's love in every possible dimension. Inheritance is bestowed upon us by God because of his love. Christianity came out of love *"for God so love the whole world that he gave his only begotten son that whosoever believe in him might not perish but have everlasting life"*.

Your response to the love of the father is what makes the love count for you. As you respond positively to every deposit of love from God, more love is shown you from him. The difference between believers and sinners is the response of the former to the love of God, which eventually led to salvation. The same response is what separates the "haves" and the "have-nots" in the kingdom of God.

In the story of the prodigal son, the two sons of the loving father misunderstood the father's love and thus messed up their inheritance. The younger one thought the father was not ready to leave the scene on time, and that the father was too slow in coming forth, so he grabbed the inheritance prematurely and squandered everything.

The story did not end there. *Jesus told it all so we can know it all.* The older brother thought the father was only interested in business so he refused to ask for anything personal even though he would have love to have a feast with his friends too and wear good robes and golden rings. He even thought the father was partial and had one rule for the younger one and another one for others. Envy and jealousy of someone making it and having it seemingly better and more than you is a reflection of the father's love misunderstood. **Luke 15:11-32.** When you understand the love of the father, you will realize that all he has are yours just as the father said to the elder son. Because you don't see it manifest yet does not mean you don't have it, for all things are yours.

The Bible is the love letter of the father sent to you. It is not a set of rules and laws to show you your failure. Your frailty was known to the father before. The word was given to help you out of it. The word was given for you to see what the father has in stock for you to become and have in spite of your shortcomings.

The Communion of the Holy Spirit

Everything that the Father has is mine. That is what I meant when I said that He [the Spirit] will take the things that are Mine and will reveal (declare, disclose, transmit) it to you...John 16:15 (Amp).

Everything God has had been transmitted to Christ Jesus. Your own portion can only reach you through the ministry of the Holy Spirit. The heaven in you is the Holy Spirit. He is the presence of God's head in you and he is the Christ living in you as the hope of glory. No one can see God the father in the flesh. Jesus died and went to heaven many years back, the evidence of God's head in us, which John the beloved invited us to fellowship with is the person of the Holy Spirit. He is not a wind but a spirit person. He came to transmit unto you what belongs to you in Godhead as inherence, in particular the aspect of it needed here on earth for you to be best that God intends you to be.

Often times, Christians want to bypass the Holy Spirit and go to God the father or Christ, so they neglect the leading of the Spirit in them while they are busy looking up in the sky for signs. The divine protocol is that whatever God the father has for you has been given to

Christ Jesus and such is being transmitted to you by the Holy Spirit. He is the headmaster and operational commander of divine activities on earth today. The essence of this first encounter Jacob had on his way into the inheritance was for him to be conscious of and give room for divine presence in his life.

The only way to benefit in what the Holy Spirit has to offer is to treat him first as a person and not a thing. Not just a person but God's person, a senior partner in your journey of inheritance.

> He is a teacher to teach you all things you need to know about your inheritance and how to appropriate it.

> He is the comforter sent to sooth you when the challenge of the land that flows with milk and honey becomes intense.

> He is the helper to help you get what is yours in spite of your human weakness or infirmity, the giants irrespective.

> He adds the super to the frailty of your natural sprit so the mixture can be supernatural and not frail again.

> He is the power generating set given to you as a standby by which you have a constant supply of energy necessary for you to function and forge ahead in your pursuits.

The relationship between you and the father of inheritance is kept fresh by the same Holy Spirit as he who sheds abroad the love of same father in your heart.

In time of physical weakness and infirmities, he revitalizes (heals and gives life to) your body so it can drive the engine of your spirit around smoothly while it lasts here on earth.

The Holy Spirit is the spirit of truth who keeps you from deceits of the world and religion so you don't miss out or derail from the path of life. Partaking of your inheritance here on earth is for the purpose of you fulfilling your assignment, otherwise you would have had to wait until you get to the millennial reign before partaking of it.

The Holy Ghost is the spirit of assignment you have received to help you fulfill purpose and finish well.

* There are many more various ways the Holy Spirit will help you be what you ought to be and have all you ought to have.

But as it is written: eye has not seen, nor ear heard, nor have entered into the heart of man the things which God has prepared for those who love Him. But God has revealed them to us through His Spirit. For the Spirit searches all things, yes, the

deep things of God. For what man knows the things of a man except the spirit of the man which is in him? Even so no one knows the things of God except the Spirit of God. Now we have received, not the spirit of the world, but the Spirit who is from God, that we might know the things that have been freely given to us by God...1 Corinthians 2:9-12

God has not only given you an inheritance but had also sent you the one who will help you "*unwrap*" it.

Kept and sealed by the Holy Spirit for the Manifestations of Your Inheritance

God said to Jacob at the beginning of this chapter that he won't be left without divine presence no matter what so he could enter all that has been spoken of him of the Lord. What could have warranted this kind of promise from the Lord should be our question seeing the man in question was a rich man's son, somewhat fulfilled to a level. The issue at hand can be better understood if we look at Jacob's state of mind at this point in time. Jacob was in fear and trepidation for his life. Evil was near in the person of his brother who vowed to avenge himself of Jacob one day while uncertainty lies ahead in moving to a strange land. It was this fear and uncertainty that led Jacob into the personal retreat that brought about this famed encounter with the God of inheritance. God vowed to preserve him, Laban and his hostile sons, Esau and his great troop irrespective.

When Cain killed his brother Abel and feared being killed in revenge, God put a seal or stamp on him to keep him from harm and he was not killed. In a similar but better and positive way has God given you the Holy Spirit as a stamp or seal over your life to enforce your safety and keeping. We saw earlier that we are kept by the power of God through faith, that power is the power of the Holy Spirit triggered by our walk of faith with him.

In Him you also trusted, after you heard the word of truth, the gospel of your salvation; in whom also, having believed, you were sealed with the Holy Spirit of promise, who is the guarantee of our inheritance until the redemption of the purchased possession, to the praise of His glory...Ephesians 1:13-14.

I love the word "*guarantee*," which is a language of faith and the mandate of the Holy Spirit on your life! Believing brings the seal or stamp of guaranteed delivery of your inheritance by the Holy Ghost. Just as in the postal system, guaranteed mail can be traced and monitored in case something goes amiss. Whenever things seem amiss in your inheritance, you can trace it by the Holy Ghost, get an update, grow in faith, and relax in assurance that it shall come to pass! One of the things the world system and religion hates about this kind of message is the "*guarantee mentality*" we have. They would rather we cringe in trepidation and lack of assurance as we face tomorrow. They would rather we say maybe, if God will, and look defeated down and out.

Some will even call it humility or fruit of the spirit if we speak the language of uncertainty, but it is not. The Holy Spirit is the spirit of guarantee, which fills us with assurance until we see the full manifestation of the possession already purchased by the faith of Christ.

Finally, I would love to say that Communion of the Holy Spirit is a product of your deliberate fellowship with the person of the Holy Spirit. It is your responsibility to allow the participation of the Holy Spirit in your daily affairs and the transportation of the Holy Ghost into your next level. All manners of prayer from petition to thanksgiving, singing to God with melody in your heart, listening and meditations in the word are the principal ways to keep the communion going. As you keep fellowshipping with him, you will be metamorphosed from one level of the glory of your inheritance to another all the days of your life until you literally become and have all that God has in place for you. At this point, stop running around, sit down with, and lay hold of your glorious inheritance in Christ and you shall find true fufilment.

The grace of the Lord Jesus Christ,
 And the love of God,
And the communion of the Holy Ghost,
Be with you.
Amen.

www.ingramcontent.com/pod-product-compliance
Lightning Source LLC
Chambersburg PA
CBHW032119090426
42743CB00007B/403